FORGOTTEN
FRAGMENTS
OF TIME

Forgotten Fragments Of Time
Copyright © 2024
DARK THIRTY POETRY PUBLISHING
ISBN: 978-1-7384128-2-2

Dark Thirty Poetry Publishing
First edition

Artwork by: Faye Alexandra Rose

DTPP23

DARK THIRTY POETRY PUBLISHING

Featuring

Ashley Roncaglione, Rheign, Harjeet Khanna, Ali
Ashhar, CLS Sandoval, Peter Cashorali, Joan
McNerney, David Thomas, Sara Sabharwal,
LaVern Spencer McCarthy, Binod Dawadi, Dr.
Robert Runté, Rex Arrasmith, Rhys Campbell,
Elijah Bean, Michael Kelleher, Micah McCutchan,
Carella Keil, Sergio A. Ortiz, Sherr Marie Diaz,
Jen Clark, Michael G. O'Connell, Jollity Archer,
Claire Thom, Angela Marie Niemiec, Dan Flore III,
Natalie Robinson, Swapna Sanchita, Jen
Colclough, Eileen Wiscombe, Darren Rankins,
L.M. Beatty, Lawrence Miles, Patricia Walsh,
Anna Ross, isaac e.j, Janis Butler Holm, Jarvis
Ottum, adam Shove, Ndaba Sibanda, Isabelle
Palerma, Kenneth Salzmann, Anita Howard,
Henry Vinicio Valerio Madriz, Ryan Kenny,
Norbert Góra, K. D. Bowers, Vanessa Caraveo, D.L.
White, E.W. Farnsworth, Tasneem Hossain, Mimi
Flood, Linda Leedy Schneider, Izzy Shackleton,
Giselle Linder, S. Bruzon, Katherinne Magaña,
Jillian Calahan, Elle Kehres, Jacek Wilkos, Zo
Copeland

Nothing that happens is ever forgotten, even if you can't remember it.

Spirited Away

FTD

Ashley Roncaglione

Left lobe deterioration.
A mental-oral misinformation.
They say language is the first to go.
What do you think I just said?
No. I did not say that at all.
Words succumb to disintegration.

My mind is not at ease.
Dis-ease of the mind.
Where is my mom?
I just want to go home.
Deaf ears lead the blind.
And home is a childlike illustration.

Am I supposed to know who you are?
I'm lacking facial recognition.
Your face is sweet, like a child.
I fail to see the correlation.
Aren't children supposed to be small?
I have almost reached my destination.

I've Been Thinking of Leaving

Giselle Linder

I've been thinking of taking a late-night cruise
from Europe to America
and watching the stars fizzle and pop over the
dark water like sparklers at a barbeque
and starting fresh there, for no other reason
except that
I can

I've been thinking of leaving you

not you, specifically, because we are in love and
the simplest rule of love is that
people who are in love don't leave each other
behind
or sometimes they do, but it haunts them to the
point that
no one really leaves each other in the end
not fully

I've been thinking of leaving all of it and every
last person
and the people they have standing beside them
too

I've spent most of my life trying to disappear and
never be found
as though, if I'm hidden long enough, everyone
will figure out how to see me
and I'll wind my way over those mountains where
people go to die

and I'll be everyone's problem but never see the
fallout
the way murderers are sometimes caught and
victims never quite are
and there are moments in your life where
everyone is fairly drawn
but it doesn't matter
because no one is ever found out

I just want to know –
how many times am I meant to die and come back
before people are tender with me?

tender in the way that people are tender with
other people, for the record
not tender in the way the butcher is with his meat

how many times am I meant to die and come
back?
I'm asking, because I can continue for as long as it
interests the both of us
and then once or twice more after it doesn't

I've been thinking of ending things
not life necessarily, not in this poem at least
but perhaps just my life – as it stands, now
in the way that I've been thinking of taking all the
things that carve out a bitter space in me
like first heartbreaks
and being seventeen on Halloween and chased by
a chainsaw-bearing Leatherface
and watching certain people you love in sanitised
white gowns wither away
and those tiny knocks of everyday life
and taking all those things and crushing them like
bugs beneath the pads of my fingers

except that I don't kill bugs

I've always been too kind
too kind, and a touch cowardly

I could end everything but I'll still be the same
fascinated by all the same things in the same
mundane ways
like tiny tattoos and Moscow mules and military
history and foreign countries
and white dresses and peeling wallpaper and
leaving home and never ever returning

I started writing poems about soldiers and quickly
gave up
I believe there are men in the world who care
more for the interior lives of those at war
than the war itself
I believe but I've never met one
I'm trying to talk about women on the homefront
and boys decaying in trenches
and how they all might perhaps have felt
but there's always a man who wants to talk about
how they invented the machine gun

I understand a little, I suppose
violence can be innovated but kindness can't be
there's always a new weapon to build, but never
really a new way of holding the door open
or of holding your friend
and people have laid on the floor together
laughing up at the ceiling
since before we were born

which is why I speak of leaving and then continue
staying, I suppose

in retro / pro -spect

Rheign

looking back
i see the tumultuous trail before me
i hear the mindless chatter around me
i feel the rising sun on my skin
i smell the hints of endless angst
i taste the broken bitterness on my tongue

where did this stem from?

looking forward
i taste the troubled tea on my lips
i smell the salty sea water in my vicinity
i feel revolutions in my bones
i hear the silent riots in the alleyways
i see glitter on the pavement

how did we get here?

repeated allusions to our own history
embedded into the essence of the hereafter.

Therapy Musings

Elle Kehres

I am a thousand different women,
Peering through a thousand different pairs of,
unfortunately near-sighted, hazel eyes,
Looking back on the thousand different lives I
have lived;
Or, I suppose you could say, lives I have lived thus
far.

It seems a little silly,
Believing myself to be so different from my past
incarnations
At the age of 28, when I'm too old to be young and
too young to be old.
Too jaded to live fearlessly
And too resigned to the fact the I most likely
won't be remembered
When I journey from this life to the next.
Or, if I do find myself lucky enough to take up
space in the afterlife,
To know that how I wish to be remembered might
not be the way you saw me.
Hell, it might not even be the way I saw me.
Does that even make sense?

If I were to die today, which version of me would
you remember?
Your childhood friend? Your first love? A love
lost?
The too-sensitive child lost in her imagination,

Or perhaps the wounded woman of my early
twenties,
Filled to the brim with dark days, starless nights,
too many cigarettes
And every cliché you can think of.

I'm asking, truly, because it appears to me that I
have lost my sense of self.
If I do not know who I am, maybe you do?
Let's just say I'm asking for a friend.

When my ashes are scattered, as requested
Across the bodies of water that felt most like
home,
What memories will you share? What stories will
live up to the sum of my experiences;
The thousand different women who have lived a
thousand different lives?

Are we seeing the same person
When I look into a mirror and, you,
Stay reaching for my hand across the table?

Am I asking too many questions?
Probably.
That must be why so much of my poetry
Ends in question marks
?

I think it comes from my endless musings in
therapy,
Trying to decipher how today's version of me fits
in
With the endless versions of her.

Am I still her?

Is she still me?
Are we destined to be less than friends;
Acquaintances, she and I?
Each incarnation amounting to
The rarely mentioned, superfluous background
details in the story of my life.

Or do I get to keep her,
Every version of her,
And love them all?
And believe that, when people think of me,
They too will see it all.

I'm doubtful. And, between you and me,
I think this less-than-pragmatic prose makes me
sound like a child,
Or maybe just a narcissist.
Or, at its core,
One damn determined woman
Attempting to reckon with her own intrinsic value
Or lack-thereof.
Nevertheless.

Take Your Pill Every Day at 8:00

S. Bruzon

I turned it off a few months ago,
abrupt vibration

ripped us away from our entanglement,
from our sweat.

from the blood
and the dust,

and the love,
and the lust,

or the need
to need
someone,
something,
a body,

a placeholder.

fingerprints
on my torso,
memory
unwind

your face buried in my hair,
memory
be
kind.

you can spit me out now.

I shut the alarm off.
It seemed to bother you.

I woke up in the afternoon
again and
mistook it for the morning.

I thought you'd like to know
I am mourning

you still.

and I continue to never do what I tell others to
and I forget to finish what I start,

I forget to turn the sadness into
art,

and I am thinking about a few people now
and how I can
take my clothes off
for them,

but tomorrow I'll only
think of myself again.

It is no joke that we can hear
this specific sound once every day,

process the buzz,
the noise,
feel the frustration,
scramble to get the pill,
perform the task,

memory,
unwind.
memory,
be kind.

forget,
forget the past.

and start over.

I shut the alarm off.
It seemed to bother you.

Tapestry of Memories

Harjeet Khanna

Amidst the echoes of time's gentle dance,
Lie memories that in our souls enhance.
In fields of nostalgia, we often roam,
In search of fragments, our heart's sweet home.

The laughter of friends in a summer's embrace,
Or the warm tears shed in sorrow's dark space.
Memories, the jewels we forever hold,
In the tapestry of life, their stories unfold.

With every sunrise and every setting sun,
New memories are born, old ones become undone.
They shape who we are, both past and today,
Anchoring us firmly, as life's tides sway.

In the quiet hours when the world's asleep,
We wander through the archives we keep.
A treasury of moments, a timeless treasure,
Each a chapter, a measure of life's grandeur.

Some memories we revisit with a smile,
While others may evoke a bittersweet mile.
Yet, in their embrace, we find a sense of grace,
As we journey through time's mysterious space.

So, let us savour each memory's hue,
For they compose a symphony of me and you.
In this symphony, life's stories entwine,
In the tapestry of memories, our souls align.

Boulevard Of Time

Ali Ashhar

Through the boulevard of time
life peeps into an era
when everything was vibrant.
A kid nascent to life dances around
the courtyard whose steps know
no onus while he runs into the garden
and hears mellifluous melodies of life
singing to him;
he comes across vibrant displays of flowers
making him fall in love with the emotions
associated.
Tired, he feels cozy sitting in the serene
shade of a tree which was planted by his parents,
with the passage of time
the vibrant flowers began
to fade away and the garden witnessed a storm
arriving.
Black clouds hover over the tree
as soon as the child turns into a man;
the vibrant flowers are withering away—
his parents are now too old to water them.

A Long Time with No Rain

CLS Sandoval

My ninth grade Spanish teacher
used to bring in her guitar
to teach us to sing
the 1969 hit, "Maria Isabel" by Los Payos

Her skin was as dry as
the Atacama Desert
of her homeland in Peru

When she sang
her voice was the dust storm
stirring up the sands
of her throat
parched from the lack of rain

Any moisture in Atacama
is only from the fogs
that dare to skim
the surface of the desert floor
no precipitation
has been recorded there
in human history

By the end of the school year
I decided
that the perfect gift
for my Spanish teacher
was a bottle of water

Memory 4

Peter Cashorali

Don't expect to take it with you,
Warning heard all through our lives.
True enough for bank accounts,
Hard drives, silver knives and forks,
Weathered grin or wrinkled brow.
But we'll take our memories,
No one will inherit those,
Like abundant furnishings
That go with us out the door,
We'll carry all those into gone,
What's not gone yet, or going now.

White Heat

Joan McNerney

This dry moment
we lay in sweat beds.

Limp flowers turned
into themselves.

Lightning scorches
skies with hot zigzags.

Will it ever rain, when
will cicadas be silent?

Memories of a white room
burning pains...shunts, stains.

A bottle bursts filling the
sidewalk with rancid beer.

Throat of bird
swollen, screaming.

Extract from Meticulous

D.L. White

Do you know what it's like? Living pill to pill, the gap between them seeming smaller and smaller, praying for tiny fractions of joy amidst the fuzz?

It's like playing a piano with someone stealing the keys. Your fingers try to touch a note but it's gone. So, you adjust, replace the note with another that's almost the same but not quite the same. You get by like that, substituting notes for different notes, the music gradually becoming discordant. The worst part is, some of keys come back; you thought they'd gone but there they are again. They come and go, but mostly go, and you do your best to make music from the mess, your head feeling like it's drowning in doubt. You wake up one day with so many keys missing that you can't even imagine how to start; so you don't. There are more and more of those days, now, with not enough keys to feel alive, let alone function.

People see me go absent – momentarily switched off – I'm not switched off, though, I'm still there, viewing the world through a tiny hole, able to observe but not interact. The hole gets smaller each time. When I return from those holes, everything is so overwhelming. Can you imagine, waking from sleep, three, five, fifteen, twenty times per day, confused and frightened, wondering how many keys were taken this time? Can you imagine that?

Imagine a tree in Autumn losing its leaves;
a message on the wind says: this is the last time.

Derelict

David Thomas

We didn't hold hands in the night.
Not anymore.
Closing our eyes
we fell away with our dreams.
One after the other.
Spinning sycamore seeds
finding their way through the rattling branches .
Leading us down
down the smooth bark
into the heartless roots
pinpointing the place all things began.
It was dark back then.
A gut twisting aching dark that courted quiet
nothingness.
But there is sound in the chaos of silence.
The downfall of a mountain.
A droning repetition of Om
wandering like the scent of lavender through an
unreachable utopia.
I only ever wanted to be strong enough
but the weight in my chest was just too much to
bear alone.
Achromatic chakras standing sentinel
floodgates sealed in stone
making a vessel of my skin.
A stagnant pool of history
a breeding pit of regurgitated emotion.
And in sudden explosions
our demons met to fight
spilling blood across the battlefield of frustration.

White noise logic drowning any wisdom before it
could coalesce.
Low light alcohol haze
emulating hate.
Flinging pain around the room as if it had no
consequence.
Spitting its molten teardrops into the rift
to burn away the foundations.
A city in ruins.
Blackout.
After all this
how could we find our way home?
Side by side.
Absent.
Lonely.
We don't hold hands in the night.
Not anymore.

Tiny Fragments of Memory

Katherinne Magaña

Time now exists only in my head,
in tiny small fragments that shine blurry like a
kaleidoscope, a kaleidoscope of memories,
Who was I before knowing the hardships of life?
who was I when all i did was blow dandelions in
the wild,
and my only hobby was to make sure the mimosas
fell asleep as the sun set.

I was nothing but a small tiny fragment of life.

Life existed long before I was a part of it, life will
continue long after I've gone. all the places I've
gone to, I think of them as a part of my life, but if I
was to depart, they'd remain; I am nothing but a
part of their life.

The stars in the sky look blurry when I lay on the
ground, I'll depart and it will not matter, the stars
will remain even long after.
I'll depart and the wind will blow the same.

A kaleidoscope of memories flies by;
  Oranges waiting for me on the table peeled by my
mother, I am 5 learning how to read.
  A musky amber-y scent of jasmines fills the air,
I am 9 and grandma is still alive- but life had to
continue even after her.
  Then I'm 12 running through forests and deserts
for a better life.

Then I'm 13 trying to speak a language that won't flow off my tongue naturally.

Now I'm 22 and my native language has mixed with the foreign.

I dream of euthanasia, dream of my body going back to its home.

How peaceful must it be! the stars will claim me back, hold my body and hold it tight.
My lungs will give one last breath and birth more dandelions
- that will remain long after I've gone.

First Frost

Sara Sabharwal

When the whimsy has worn
And the sparks have long faded—
Our butterflies have turned to dust,
Same as the stars that once glittered in your eyes,
Will memories be enough to sustain?
Can smoldering embers be enough
Or will we freeze one another out
As we reach for blankets instead of one another?

A Mother Remembers

LaVern Spencer McCarthy

A mother prays, remembering her son
who died in battle on a rugged shore.
She often sits and weeps when day is done.

She does not care if war was lost, or won.
She only wants to hold him as before.
A mother prays, remembering her son.

Tonight, when steeple bells had just begun
to ring, she thought she heard him at the door.
She often sits and weeps when day is done.

She needs a sign. Her moments have been spun
from joy to tears. Her heart is sick and sore.
A mother prays, remembering her son.

She longs to die, that she might gladly run
through Paradise to see his face once more.
She often sits and weeps when day is done.

She hopes for peaceful hours, but there are none,
only her loss that nothing will restore.
A mother prays, remembering her son.
She often sits and weeps when day is done.

Eidolon

David Thomas

There was a pause
for the briefest of moments.
I could hear the walls creak
before they began to close in
breathless.
And the fears plummeted like a falcon
burning up on entry
spreading wildfire
through clogged synapses.
Head turns in slow motion
to greet those burned witches
still casting curses in all their tangled threads.
The cord is corrupted
tearing its way through the mill where we first
ran from monsters.
It was the thick of it
the footprints still marked our tender skin.
It was supposed to be something else
something stronger
but the damage was already done.
It seems that threads don't break so easily.
And as the volume increases
from silence to a song
as time comes back to life
I find tragedy in the dream.
It could have been yesterday
it could have been last night.
But it wasn't.
Holding the lyrics in my hands
trying to catch the liquid of their agony

molten.
But I am numb
faded
extinguished
forgetting all the things that crave a transition
into ash.

I'm Glad We Didn't Get Married

Giselle Linder

I never stopped loving you, and I'm glad we didn't
get married

I'm glad I stopped holding your hand to make sure
you wouldn't get lost
And instead slipped my bare feet through the
Southern fog
And pressed my back to the tiled floor of that
barren quarter home
Instead of waiting by your backdoor like a lover,
like a reaper
Like a dog

I was raised in such a sullen way so as to want
you
Whether you were swaying on two feet or down on
one knee
But there were days where I longed for more than
your repentance
I'm too much, more than half of what you wanted
me to be

I don't say yes or no to you
I've got no cause to lie
When the time comes no questions are asked
We've got great cause to die

I've been carrying such heavy suitcases, even
Sisyphus would ask why

I wouldn't call a spade a spade on the burden of
your company
I've always been too shy

We can play out the fullness of conversation –
You say Hello and I'll say Goodbye

Am I your lover, or are you mine?
I never stopped wanting you but I'm glad we
didn't get married
You were half of all goodness in the world
You're another thing I'll live to see buried

I don't want to see you long lost
I don't want to see you gone
But you're sweating through these white cotton
sheets
And I was raised in such a sullen way so as to
always move on

You may open the creaking door under wavering
moonlight
And slip through the wheels of time down under
Swann's way
I'll tell you to meet me tomorrow night

And then I'll leave today

Memory Loss

Dr. Robert Runté

We perceive our selves
who we are,
in this moment,
as the culmination of all our experiences;
therefore: that our memories are a part of us,
something that we have,
or that we lose
as we forget.

But memory is also held for us by others.
The people who know who we are,
because they were there
and remember too.

Their memory, perhaps,
ever so slightly different,
a variant perspective,
as if seen from an angle
to where we thought
we remembered standing.
Recognizable, still, as the same moment.

Defining moments,
existing in our heads, our selves. . .
infinitely outnumbered
by the memories held in trust by others
remembering those same moments.
Mirrors to our remembered selves.

What happens when those others are gone?

What happens to our selves when they leave
and in leaving,
take some portion of our memories with them?

Unbalanced,
more of our memories
across that boundary
than remain here,
we begin to lean, to tip precariously,
until inevitably,
we are our selves
forgotten.

The Ghosts (of Childhood) Live in the Wall of my Grandma's House

Sara Sabharwal

My grandmother stoops over our small heads,
Ruler in one hand pen in the other.
Our favorite holiday tradition—
As we compete with one another.
Dark ink lines blare boldly against white paint
While years past fade to soft gray.
Comparing our heights as if it was a race—
Who grew the most.
In a way,
It was.
The naivety of youth
Always wanting to be grown.
Not understanding that time is limited.
We stand on tiptoe, hoping she doesn't notice.
But the playful tap of the ruler on our heads
reminds us we can't get anything by her.
She understands.
She remembers all too well the desire to grow up.
Move on to the next thing,
And she did.
It all happened faster than she could ever
imagine.
Her mind flashes back to a more chaotic time
When no one called her grandma—
But four wild things called her mama.
When they too stood tip toe,
Backs against the same wall.
Their faded ink lines intertwined with ours.

Tick tock
Our parents rejoice as we meet and exceed their
lines—
Bittersweet.
They too know all too well,
Time is a thief.
We blink
And our entire lives are different.
We grow up,
Only then realizing how precious childhood was.
In your case,
Childhood was all you'd have.
Yellow daisies with black centers
Still remind me of you
And every time I see porch swing,
I'm transported back—
Grandmas front porch
Country roads
Black eyed Susan bushes.
You laughed harder than anyone I'd met.
It's almost like you knew 19 short years is all
you'd get.
The world continues to spin
Leaving our childhood in the dust,
The bushes have been dug out,
The wooden swing rotted away,
And the height wall long painted over,
But you're still there—
6 years old and beaming
Standing on tiptoes to grow up sooner.
Oh if I could tell you
"Just stay here"
We will swing a little longer
Even after she hollers that supper is ready.
We'll make daisy chains and flower crowns,

Place them on our heads and wear them around
until the petals dry out and turn to dust.
But alas,
Time offers no return
A moment gone is forever lost.

In memory of Timothy Steil

Sixty and eight

Rex Arrasmith

I remember when my father's mother [turned]
sixty and eight
In 1973. My grandmother seemed so olde then
and needed help
Getting around.

She was one year away from being placed in a
place for olde
People. She couldn't be left on her own. She'd left
the burner on
In her kitchen, then scalded herself in the
bathtub.

I was eighteen. I had been living with her, helping
her out.
I wasn't always patient, and I was ashamed when
I found her
In her tub, blistered and shivering, unable to get
out.

Today I turned sixty and eight. I can't help
thinking about
My olde addled grandmother. Wearing a paper
crown, her
Chignon askew, sitting confused among the
mayhem.

I'd wanted to celebrate her birthday, she sat
surrounded by

Her family, her wheelchair decorated. I'd had to help her
Dress for the party, she was happy.   I was resentful.

Why was she, my responsibility? Now that I am her age then,
Childless, I guess I'm happy I won't have to be a burden.
To an impatient grandchild.

And yet, here I sit with my partner, in good health on my 68th.
I still feel guilty for my internal resentment. I did what I was
Asked, I was a good boy, and   I loved her.

But at the time, I was relieved when she was sent away to die alone
In a [retirement home] where she was neglected by her care givers
and me.
Even now I hate how I felt, how we treated her.

After she died, I dreamt for years about how I'd go to that place,
And rescue her. In dreams, she would become her old self. She'd
Make me breakfast, tell me stories, drink coffee and whiskey,
Out of an old china cup.

Wish It All Away

D.L. White

I find it strange;
this addiction to next season—
wishing away the wonder of today
for a recycled promise of tomorrow.
As if each single second isn't just as precious as
the next.
As the first.
As the last.
Whether basked in sunshine
or making angels in snow.
Sweeping fallen leaves
or watching them grow.
Do dying leaves offer more peace
than young buds—
because we fear the uncertainty of new things
more than we fear certain death?
Or, are we sick of watching pretty things live
such fleeting fragile lives—
Thinly ripened fruit;
sweet on the tongue
bitter in the gut.
Spit them out
and start again,
whilst the thickness of death
slithers endlessly on.

Can a kiss from Winter winds
press from heavenly lips?
Can flapping Summer wings
blow holes in the universe?

For, what is Summer without Winter—
What is Autumn without Spring?
What is any one thing without the other?

There are no seasons
to love and grief—
they freeze and thaw our hearts
at all times.
On temperate or tempestuous days;
Through howling rains
or blistering drought.
A heart may break for falling leaves
As much as heal for their purpose.

What if you found love in April,
held it close through May;
took a grieving knee in August—
In September,
Would you wish it all away?

Memories Dissipate

Rhys Campbell

The moon will turn its face
In time, another half will fade
We develop a reliance on our loved ones' grace
And it's so easy to be left with a bitter taste
Believing the imprint was a waste

Dwell and be honest
Otherwise, you'll regret it when you want it
It's so easy to be complacent
When you've become compliant
To the lingering black noise

Pressure builds to the surface
When the reminder of mortality
Emerges dissident
And the sun doesn't set at all
When faced with one's innocence
In cold and rough skin

A lingering silhouette
That's no longer filled with regret
Anguish and torment may come out to play
But love was always here to stay
When our memories have faded away

Nova Kraisalis

Elijah Bean

Closing my eyes now
My heart is at rest
All is ever so calm
Like the surface of a lake at twilight
I am sleepy
I want to dream
Drawn in, as a magnet unto metal
I fall into my chest
A torus, within my breasts
Leave me here
Neath the wings of Luna
I am asleep
I am awake in a dream
And it is
O' so beautiful.

Chloe's Desire at Last

E. W. Farnsworth

Hair wild, auburn tinged blood red,
She turned to the side to see her svelte figure.
Sultry, undersexed and overly admired,
No love of her life to fulfil her dreams,
No dreams, really, except of Charon waiting
By the still, black water.
As she rocked and fantasized, a male army passed
Her strictest review, and Charon smiled.
His muffled oars rowed blind souls in silence.
But Chloe hungered and thirsted still.
It hurt her head to number eves like this,
Feeling the end was near.
He came in a rush and boated her
And held her through the tempest of her soul.
Then as she saw the far shore in dawn light,
Her smiling lover draped her with a shroud.
She wondered about desire and whether
At last she had been truly satisfied.
Her long fingers touched his cold smiling face
As his boat slid onto the far shore.
There her mind went black as midnight.
Her body felt a chill.
Was this the end or the beginning?
Charon, discreet, would never tell.

Ask Me

Linda Leedy Schneider

Ask me if I speak for the peony.
and I will tell you, yes.
I speak for green veined
leaves, the fuchsia flower that burns
like the heart of a ballet dancer.
I speak for fecund heaviness, and peony's love
and fear of lightning. I speak for all
with one chair at their table
whose heads are full of moon jelly.
Current moves swiftly not like the snail,
and to blossom can be a burden.

Yes, I speak for the peony
loved in her youth for her beauty
Then cut down as she crinkles and sags.
But, next year a fuchsia fist
will plunge through the soil,
and peony will begin again
if she is allowed just water and sun.
I speak for our waning water,
the moon, our sister,
the sun, mother of us all.
Yes, I speak for the peony.

A Day In The Life Of A Four Year Old

Michael Kelleher

Stand there by the door stay quiet and wait,
when the milkman arrives go to the gate.
I look to the field and acres of gorse
and see O'Shea with his cart and his horse.
Four pints if you would, sir, straight from the urn,
just past the eggs and butter you churn.
He was nearly as quick as me, you see,
Nearly as quick as me.

From the gate to the house must be a mile.
I can sing a song and manage a smile.
In a few steps my tune starts to stutter,
my palm being sliced by a cheese cutter.
The weight of the task lay on young shoulders,
this thing in my hand is a great boulder
It was nearly as large as me, you see,
Nearly as large as me.

Shooed out of the way and in the main room,
Nan sweeps away with her wicked witch broom.
Grandad tells me some more stories of old.
asks me to stop talking, don't be so bold.
He tries to chase me round the huge table.
Never caught me, although he was able.
He was never as fast as me, you see,
Never as fast as me.

Uncle John's home and we're walking the dogs,
we're running through fields and leaping the logs.
We picked the berries that reach for the sky,
our hopes for Nan's special blackberry pie.
We went home slowly, took care not to trip,
the dogs kept trying to give us the slip.
They were nearly as tall as me, you see,
Nearly as tall as me.

We got home and put the berries in store,
the cabinet shelf reached down for the floor.
The smell of fresh butter, tea and some ham
invaded our nostrils, as did the spam.
With a flourish Nan sliced doorsteps of bread,
great lashings of jam, giant dollops of spread.
It was nearly as big as me, you see,
Nearly as big as me.

On the floor, Nan filled the massive tin bath
I played with my toys and had a great laugh.
Hot water was nice but made me quite red.
Come little one it's now time for your bed.
As she tucked me in, Nan stifled a yawn,
to care for us all she'd get up at dawn
She was as nearly as tired as me, you see,
Nearly as tired as me.

Family Album

Jacek Wilkos

family album
gazing from old photographs
faces of strangers

Why Not?

Micah McCutchan

today is someone's birthday
somewhere there are crinkly star shaped
balloons kissing the ceiling of a warm dining
room, candles melting into cool whip,
bleeding their color into iced writing.
somewhere there is laughter, somewhere
someone is turning 10 or 16 or 27 or 99.
somewhere someone is telling someone
they love them for the first time,
hands touching under a white tablecloth,
promises made through eyelashes & shoulder
shrugs.
somewhere someone is learning to spell
their name for the first time,
tracing the letters just right,
finding themselves in crayon or clay or dark ink
pen.
somewhere someone is being born,
taking their first wonderful & terrifying breath,
becoming.
somewhere someone is being returned to the
earth,
using their last breath to assure those
who love them that they are finally going home.
somewhere someone is celebrating
why not me? why not you?

Take Me Home to My Baby

Tasneem Hossain

Who are you? Can you tell me true?
Where is my baby? Please bring her to me.
This is me, mom your daughter Sue.
Look at me, hold me tight. Sit safely.

Where is my baby? Please bring her to me.
My head is a buzz. Don't make a fuss.
Look at me, hold me tight.Sit safely.
Are you the nurse? Please bring my purse.

My head is a buzz. Don't make a fuss.
Why is everything so hazy?
Are you the nurse? Please bring my purse.
It's me, mom, your baby. Don't be so hasty.

Why is everything so hazy?
Please take me home to my baby girl Sue.
It's me, mom, your baby. Don't be so hasty.
Who are you? Can you tell me true?

Looking At My Brother's Photograph

LaVern Spencer McCarthy

I was washing dishes the day
my brother was slapped into the army.
Smirking and bold, loaded with
eighteen years of belligerence,
he was lounging at the kitchen table
bad-mouthing my uncle, not there to defend
his teacherous ways.

Mother, always handy with water-blistered
knuckles,
knocked Harold all the way
to the recruiter's office.
Afterward, a Greyhound bus
propelled his furious momentum
toward boot camp.

He returned two years later
body-bagged and silent, all rebellion
lost in a rice paddy somewhere in Viet Nam.
Mother cried, but I stood at his coffin
angrily plucking petals
from his spray of long-stemmed roses,
wondering how he came to be dead
from a single slap.

Cotton Candy Sunset

Carella Keil

Originally published by Flora Fiction Vol. 4 Issue 2

Dreams mingle with the porcelain of reality.

I wonder how many protoplanets were ground up
to make my coffee, as the bangles I stole from
Saturn cascade down my wrist.

You are what you eat. I'll take the yolks of
universes, an event horizon, the frosting off an
iced galaxy. I wait impatiently for the other guests
to arrive, digesting meteorites and flossing stars
from between my teeth.

Garden of Poets and Papers

Sergio A. Ortiz

You used to origami into my hammock
late at night in Playa del Carmen —remember
me reciting obligatory prayers
in the mornings?

At night, spooning, kisses, tenderness,
we'd turn on the furnace.

I never asked about your business.

You'd take care of the cat while I was ironing
out my fears. There was an epidemic.
People were dying.

I was scared and angry, conscious of the new
chains
around my neck. Winter blared
its apocalyptic voice. It felt like when I watched
someone get a blow job
in Central Station. Too much danger, not my
tango.
I sniffed scum and walked out.
I prefer waiting for your Mayan
dances on my prostate.

My ocean was once alive.
It sang songs, andante
melancholy verses dedicated
to Julia, his spirit guide.

Its voice was beaten to death.
Caution, it raises like a vampire
from its thumb when angered,
feasts on your fears.
It's a carnivorous cunt,
treacherous if pressured.

Can still cook up a spell or two in the mirror.
That dick-eating beast leaves footprints
around his mother's womb,
her diamond covered mask.

Eternal Sunshine of The Spotless Mind

Mimi Flood

Can you remember the night at the beach ? We
went skinny dipping in late March. My heart was
speeding, and you held me through the waves.
Time goes by fast when you're happy. Through
webbed moons and the forgotten appeal who we
once were when we fell. Are we trying to tell
ourselves that we're good. Living through each
pleasing memory after the other. Should we just
become ghosts, and if we ever see each other
again, it will feel like a haunting. But before we let
go.

I just want to say

I'm going to ......

Try to remember everything

I am lost

Sherr Marie Diaz

In the midst of the night
A bolt of lightning strike
Like a swift of air
Stealing something precious in my mind
The memories I cherish
Is now floating somewhere
Just like that...my memory is gone
I don't know where I am
Or who I am
I am so confused
People calling me
How do they know me
My head spinning
Feeling adrift in the wilderness
No recollection of the present nor the past
All I know...
I am now forever loss
With no sense of reality..

What Is A Memory?

Jillian Calahan

Wrinkled clock hands
reach through my chest
plucking at strings
beneath my ribs.
A haunted lullaby
escapes from behind
my gated teeth.
And after all,
what is a memory

but time's ghost?

15 years

Jen Clark

15 years since I've seen your face
or heard you laugh
Singing hymns at the kitchen sink
Cleaning up after everyone
with a smile on your face
Family gatherings were
your happy place
15 years since the last reunion
Nobody sees each other anymore
Some may blame the decades of time passed
People just change I guess but
you brought everyone together
Every holiday was an event
and labor of love
Up at 3am to shred the cabbage for the slaw
Before even making a hot breakfast for us
The little ones that called you Nanny
A grandmother who hung the stars
You were a second mother
Stepping in when your own daughter was sick
Teaching us to read
Driving us to school
While praying the Lord's Prayer along the way
Reminding us about what matters most
Faith
Family
Love
15 years
It's been so long
Yet it feels like yesterday

that you left us
15 years.

Almost Life, Almost

Michael G. O'Connell

To visit you today means
that I will once again become your
grandson, husband, or nurse.
But on a good day—an increasingly rare day—
your son.

Now, I think of all the things I might have been.
Is that cold? Am I being selfish?

As if broken bones could hurt more
than the names that they used on me.
That the ache of loneliness could somehow
hurt less than the fall you took
putting a cast on your broken arm—
bringing you the attention you crave.
Not that your craving demanded attention,
you just loved people.
The people you are now leaving
a little more each day.

How many times? How many ways?
Was I supposed to go first?
Was I even supposed to be here?

The man in the red corvette convertible
didn't think so.
I was young and aggressive and I passed him
just to gain an extra fifty feet.
Fifty feet and I almost lost my life

because we both wanted to be first—had to be first.
And I robbed him of it. And to think, for that,
he wanted my life.
Was it my youth or something else?
Bang! Bang! Maxwell.

Do you remember the Memorial Day party
on the river bluff in your backyard?
You know that house never felt like home to me.
How could it?
You moved there without telling me.
Remember?
That day, we were all drinking way too much,
as usual, and Dad wanted, needed me
to do him a favor. It was always a favor.
That was his way.
"Climb up there," he said pointing at the mast
on our Hobie Cat. "Replace that cable."
I was too drunk to realize it then, but that cable
was the one that held everything in place.
I rarely questioned him and talked with him less.
And like that particular cable, he was the one
who held everything together.
That realization came too soon and too late.
"They'll want to use the Hobie," he said. 'They.'
It was always about the others.
I have that, too. Got it from both of you.
So I shimmied and tried.
And failed.
Too tired and too weak to get the job done.
Perhaps it was the hand of God
trying to keep me from my doom?
But you—you, always with the words
of encouragement and praise. You urged me
to keep trying. So, I put the channel locks

in my mouth, like a pirate, and went for it,
and almost died when I pulled the pin
that held the mast in place.
It's funny now—
funny like "Wile E. Coyote. Genius." is funny.
He, too, should have died when he
went over the cliff.

It is the guilt now haunts me.
More than the time my college roommate
put his rusty old gun to my head.
He claimed the mafia was after him.
If true, who could blame him?
He had gotten caught up in some kind
of conspiracy. Real or imagined, it didn't matter.
For months he had no money to pay his bills
or rent or to buy anything to feed himself
so he helped himself to mine. S'funny how he
always had enough for his two-pack-of-cigarettes
and case-of-beer-a-day habit. So he raged and
threatened and he pleaded
for his life as he placed the barrel to my temple
and pulled back the slide—
laughing and crying.

I have learned to live with that ghost, I hear it
whispering in my ear to remember.
'Remember when the light was red.
When the road ahead was clear
but the intersection was not.'
I know I shouldn't have survived
when I closed my eyes,
dropped my hands from the steering wheel,
and pushed the gas pedal to the floor.
I wanted to fly like an eagle. To leave this place.

And I did.
I was airborne for the briefest of moments,
but I was flying with angels.
Looking back, I don't reflect on the how I made it
through the intersection untouched,
it is the why.

There is so much I never told you.
These stories barely scratch the surface,
but I know, even now, with you living
amongst the ravages of your mind,
so much of my life would destroy you.

The ringing in my ears is loud now.
Is it damage? Age? Both?
Like a jet engine roars just before it gets
the go ahead from the control tower to take off,
and yet, I can still hear the words.
The ones that told me I did everything right—
your overwhelming and, at times,
smothering pride and love.
Even when I failed.
I sit here, at your bedside day after day,
helpless to do anything but watch.
All I can do is wave the doctors off as you wished
and wait for you to die—
ever the good son.

Some days I fool myself and can almost believe
I did my best.
And on some days—increasingly abundant days—
I know what I could have done.

Always.
Words of encouragement,
words of love.

Old Friends

Peter Cashorali

Once the ocean takes something
Best to let it just be gone.
Better to catch the last perfume
Of a long-vanished friend
And exhale the ache
Than to meet a dull stranger
With grandchildren for coffee sometime,
To train your palate to the sugars and tannins
Of everything being irreplaceable,
As if you'd been born falling
From some high place you'd never seen
And everything around you was falling as well.
We never meet one another again—
We're that river that can't be
Stepped in twice.
I loved you once and while I did
Loved you forever.

One Of One

Jollity Archer

Our paths always entwine
too long have we danced
One final time I witness
as we warp, writhe, unwind
You think my heart, yours
eternally beats to your tune
Alas, the song is over
now we only share the moon

What We Did in the Dark

Rex Arrasmith

I didn't have the words, only the uncomfortable
feelings. What were they? Longing, envy, lust?
There was definitely lust. Did you know?
Undoubtedly, you were—shameless. We were
inseparable. You must have known...

I remember we'd laugh and scream the lyrics
when the Lovin' Spoonful rhymed groovy with old
time movie. I 'd go to sleep at your house playing
Gordon Lightfoot like a mantra in my dreams.
Didn't you know?

> If you could read my mind, love
> What a tale my thoughts could tell

We'd spend hours playing board games, then after
midnight I'd talk you into streaking the
neighborhood. It was easy talking you out of your
clothes. You were proud of your body. You knew I
liked to look at you—you had to know.

We'd sneak back into your parent's den naked and
giggling and shivering. In a fort of blankets, we
snuggled into each other, a perfect spoon. You
pretended not to care how handsy I was. Oh, how I
loved you. I wanted you to know.

Then—betrayal, at seventeen you got a girlfriend,
so I got a girlfriend. Two Linda's, mine a beard. I
knew what to do with my Linda, I'd already

practiced everything with you. Your Linda liked
having me around, I wonder what she knew.

My Linda didn't last, I was grateful to her,
sleeping with a girl meant I wasn't a virgin? You
were thrilled—relieved? We smoked pot and
congratulated each other. After graduation,
different colleges in different states, I knew I'd
miss you.

By then I knew who I was, what I wanted. Away
from you I found it—them. We spoke on the phone,
and for the first time you heard my lies, you
believed my easy lies. I knew you knew my she's
were he's. We both knew.

We never talked about what we did in the dark.

Water Dragons

David Thomas

I don't remember much of life before this.
I don't remember much of anything.
There was laughter and sunshine
and plans for a future.
Slow beach walks
into perfect amber sunsets.
Watching cormorants posing
water dragons with open arms
on slick black breakwater posts.
There were dizzy tequila days
straddling either side of twilight
staggering through the balmy darkness into
unconsciousness.
There was no need for hope
no need for tears
but the intricacies slip through my fingers
in the way that dreams momentarily linger.
Am i even awake?
I am so far from the familiar
and with every lurch of my aching heart
I find myself a little more alone.
The sudden drops are so steep
I doubt I'll ever crest the waves of these memories
again.
I pine for the contentment of ignorance
for the untelling of tales
for the paint to run from the canvas.
But the past is set in stone
epitaphs and monuments to the figments i
thought were real.

It has burned at me
acid guilt for a life unlived
and yet here it lies spreadeagled before me
waiting.
I don't remember much of life before this
but i recognise the signposts that point to a place
far from here.
That bury me in memory.
That take me home.

Buried Treasure

Claire Thom

Three fish eyes in a row
set in tiny crowns.
Etched forever in gold,
initials of a woman I didn't really like
and a gentle man I never knew.
Wrapped around
my own ring finger now.

When my mother's mother died,
I should have cried
but my eyes couldn't
find appropriate tears.
In her closing years,
dementia made her more malleable,
as if she couldn't remember
how to be mean anymore.

Many years before,
he had dropped dead
at the front door.
Heart just stopped.
The embarrassment and inconvenience
she said it caused her
in front of the neighbours
said it all.

Diogenes syndrome transformed her
house into a museum,
displaying a life story
desperately in need of a curator.

Fur coats and handmade dresses
never worn,
squirreled away.

The nursing home staff found her
adorable. I hardly recognised her
without the ghastly wig.
She finally let my mum
comb soft, white hair
hidden underneath for years.

Dill

Ashley Roncaglione

My favorite memory isn't really a memory—
it's a smell.

A scratch-n-sniff pickle sticker that
I got at the state fair with my grandfather.

Is a feeling stronger than a memory?
Because I felt happy holding his hand
yet I don't recognize my own face.

If I inhale hard enough
will your molecules imbed into my brain?

Then long after the memory of you is gone
maybe the scent will still remain.

Shifting Sands

Angela Marie Niemiec

Falling through the hourglass
Sliding quickly from my grasp
Nowhere to even catch a breath
Along the surface without a scratch.

Cascading moments intertwine
Tumbling fragments equate the time
Passing along without hesitation
Collecting into a heavy pile.

We're running out of borrowed sand
Cycling through the narrow band
Where is the beginning
Where is the end
I'm dizzy again
There goes the last grain...

And all is gone in a blink.

Hex on the Beach

Izzy Shackleton

Every second I spend awake
Is another spool of wire drawn
And magnetic tape cut
The limits and bounds of the system decaying
And here there is no deep storage under Svalbard
I can't quite recall my first words
I hope they were simple and I was healthy
But I remember eating stones
And breaking my teeth
And pulling all the dirt from the bones of the
earth
And wanting to become rock before the world

I would say the times of woe stick deep in my
mind
Like an arrowhead
Or a falling shard of skyscraper glass
But the pain is smooth now
I remember the hurt but not the hurting
The sting remains but not the stinger
The memory died to give me this ache
And occasionally an allergic reaction

We are sorry to announce that the mental service
to your dreams have been cancelled
Due to a shortage of interest
And a lack of working history
On your CV/mental record
What happened in 2016? 17?
Were you happier then or bored?

Were your unfilled bra cups your saviour
Or the sword you ran against yourself?

I shudder at the thought of the dead teen and the
never living man
Who walk in pace with my shadow
Their beards as long as forearms
And their minds full of sand
The waves crash against my feet and beg me to
drown
As all things do eventually
Whether in space or a sound off the coast of
Scotland
We swim and swim and dive
Until the air runs out
But I look at the sand-mud and don't even sigh
I'm sinking besides my sundress curls
And legs I deforested
I think back to the toddler and ask if he'd eat
seashells
If nacre was as delectable as silica or cotton
Or if the carbon monoxide was too high a proof in
my house
And the dead ones have been forgotten.

Stewart Melprat And His Cadillac

Dan Flore III

Stewart Melprat
just drove by
in a shiny, new Cadillac

Stewart Melprat is dead
but he sure looks good now
in that Cadillac

it's so pretty
even the sun is afraid to touch it

Memory 3

Peter Cashorali

Bookcases are full, attic is full.
Sooner or later everything
Holds hands with everything else.
Time to enjoy things or time
To throw things away? Yes.
For a minute this morning I disappeared.
In dreams my first husband who died
And my husband I live with
Are the same husband.
Why is this a mystery?
Isn't that boy with his library books still here,
The one no one saw again,
His name evaporated like wine, like perfume, like
what?

Cardinal

Natalie Robinson

When I came out of the black, he was dead.
Blood on my hands. Bloodied fingers. Splay them
out in front of me:
Red feathers, rare bird
Look at them
See what I have or have not done

When I came out of the black
She was gone
Red smeared
Crossbody
The shape of
Hands or wings

On Meeting School Friends After Years

Swapna Sanchita

We walk a little slower now...
And do not let ourselves push each other over the
edge,
With too many awkward whys and hows and why
nots.
We've learnt to stop mid conversation and walk
away
From everything that bristles, hurts, and tires us
out.
We listen with our faces, having schooled our eyes
To reveal just the right amount of concern, to
prevent
Bearing witness to a moment when the curtains
are drawn.
We wake up too early, sleep too late
We reach out too often for stronger coffee, a stiffer
drink,
Our minds constantly preoccupied with our own
struggles
Which now that we are older, we forget how to
share,
But these secrets that aren't... we still let slip
though
In unguarded moments that we deign to disguise
in laughter.
Our hairs are thinner with far too many greys.
We no longer pretend, but we still hide in so many
tiny ways.

We find prettier, sweeter, kinder words for each other,
While we search for the person we used to know,
And sometime in the a.m., piled into a silly giggly heap,
We find who we used to be.

Just Maybe

Eileen Wiscombe

I remember the man you were
Spoke often yet soft spoken
Witty with a sense of practicality
Smart as a whip and quick with a quip
Loving with a side of respect
Family man extraordinaire
Then one day you weren't there
It was only a short little blip
But oh how it made our hearts dip
Time had now become our most precious
commodity
And at the same time our worst enemy
The race was now on against the clock
What started out slow with a glitch here and there
Rapidly declined to a heartbreaking stare
You are now lost in a world all your own
And man what I'd give to bring you back home
To be able to tell you what an impact you've been
And to tell you how much to us all you do mean
Though it seems time has won
And the chances are gone
I'll keep trying and hoping
For I know you are strong
And maybe, just maybe
You'll find your way back again
Because even just a moment
Would be everything.

Gabriel

Jen Colclough

If Autumn is the most beautiful death,
then winter is its haunting.
A ghostly period on which
     to
          hang
              bows,
the decorative corpses
of a different season.

July and August are dead
— you killed them.
You light a cigarette beneath a
streetlamp,
     knowing this.
Two lights,
though unequal,
flicker on the edge of dawn.

What separates angels from ghosts is beauty.
     To be haunted
          is to be cared for in reverse.

To feel so loved by an absence
     that you fear it.

In a dream, I tell you this:

That on our knees we beg for angels,
while ghosts come to us
willingly.

Angels are beautiful because we cannot touch
them.
Ghosts are hideous because
      they can touch us,
      and they do.

Above us,
the lamplight flickers out.

      [God is blinking.]

The difference between ghosts and angels is
beauty.
A dying man thinks Gabriel is gorgeous,
but a dead man thinks the beauty lies with us.
That's why they cannot look away—
      the ghosts.
They miss the way our bones
      are hidden on the insides of ourselves,
            still awaiting burial.

            And history,
you mutter beneath your smoking hand.
            Ghosts have a history,
            but angels do not need to.
            Perfection cannot bear to have a
past.

I'm always forgetting that part.

The part about time becoming us.

The Memories of Yesterday

Darren Rankins

The memories of yesterday were the times we
played, the days I came around just to see the
smile on your face and how your smile told me
why the sun shines.

The memories of yesterday were the rainbows
that I could never express,
the way you made me feel.
But to me, you were a living soul.

The memories of yesterday
are like thoughts today—loving, holding,
and waiting to be with you,
knowing all my dreams
will come true.

The memories of yesterday remind me of the last
day I spent with you, I cried for the simple reason
that I cared. Please remember me always. Your
loving friend.

Permanence

L.M. Beatty

There's nothing quite so diametrically opposed
    in a world of finites. And yet,
there are few concepts which we both crave
    and fear for the marks it leaves
    on our bodies and souls.
Permanence.

Would love last to eternity and beyond
    as the stories promise us?
Would fame follow us all the way to an end
    where even death wouldn't allow reprieve?
Would wealth carry our dreams and burdens
    through generations with no regard
    for skill or merit?
Would honor give us a worthy seat at every
    table so we could receive endless glory?
Would health keep us strong & supple so that
    never would we miss a memory
    due to illness or ache?

These are ideals, yet we live in a world of ideas;
    a dimension in which the journey matters
    more than the destination.
To achieve permanence would mean
    sacrificing life. Time would be frozen
    and void of connection.
To move and breathe and laugh and cry
    requires fluidity—not just that in a droplet
    of water—but of the tremendous tidal waves
    crashing in the middle of a stormy sea.

We can't find permanence here and, ultimately,
    we wouldn't know what to do with it.
Better to live in the flux. Better to live
    with an open hand.
Let the experiences come and go.

The permanence of forever is somewhere else.

Only Yesterday

Lawrence Miles

I still remember it
We were all in our friend's driveway
Hanging out
I remember sitting at a table but I don't remember
what we were doing
Probably nothing but shooting the breeze
You got up
You had to go
I remember you walking up the driveway
Back to your house
I can see the colors of the sky
The color of the concrete of the sidewalk
The color of the clothes you were wearing
At the time I just went back to
Whatever I was doing
Probably nothing but shooting the breeze
I never saw you again
Every so often
I go back to that time and place
Like it was only yesterday
Because one time
I might have the chance to say to you
Don't go.

(for Gary)

In the Morning

Linda Leedy Schneider

Open the love window, Rumi says,
and close the language door.
Today I look through my window
and see a cardinal feed seed to his mate
next to a mandevilla vine that carries pink
trumpets,
wraps itself around my porch railing,
climbs the column, holds her flowers to the sun.
Clings, hangs on for life.

I opened the love window 55 years ago,
and now he is gone.
His ashes are in a blue urn to my right.
I could turn my head and look at him,
but I look to the feeder,
the maple leaves full of hands,
the mandevilla vine that clings,
pink with the joy of life.

I was her once, but now I no longer cling.
I had to close the love window
and open the door to language.
I miss his hands, his deep voice,
the way he touched my back in crowds,
his laughter and the way he would sing to birds
and they would answer him.
Sometimes I still hear him sing

in the morning through the closed love
window.

Not For Individual Resale

Patricia Walsh

Making up for found time, a pleasure for me
Hating the opposition with heartfelt cause
Walking the gauntlet in pure derision
A theory on situation misses and hits decisively
A joke if not tragic, a sleeping curse.

Taking by surprise, the hard quips sink in
No apposite kiss, better to go home
The festering day-to-day needing some form
A very fashionable culture eating it's innards.

Contacting the betters, bringing the little ones
home
Productivity being lowered, stunning times
Stealing through research, a studied imagination
Flayed advertisement a key on giving
The need for entertainment awaits, in arms.

Departmental askance, taking questions like this,
Rubbed the wrong way, a failure discerning
Education being tasty, a mound of coverage
Fixed assets insulting to the hireath in charge.

Taking the creases out of the superannuated
No one quite like a superior love, perhaps
Cemented over coffee, a smoky fact
Representing alma mater's on field trips
Sorely not regretting the song gone before.

A Lonely Heart

Darren Rankin

Alone in an unforgiving sea,
my hand reaches deep
into darkness for your reach,
until water parts.
Standing on a mountain,
searching as far as the eyes can see.
Salty tears descending
upon a beating heart.
Never to be abandoned,
sunset near as snowstorm approaches.
The search must continue,
because I love you.

Jetsam

Anna Ross

I wash ashore, I don't know where.
Feeling land beneath my body.
                    Where am I?

I open my eyes to white sands.
As the waves give their last caress,
                    Why so bright?

I recall a sickness in me,
And the water was cold, so cold.
                    Am I dead?

I prise my hands from the debris,
Coughing up salt water and bile.
                    Is this home?

I clutch my head, then I remember,
They took an ear, before jettison.
                    Proof of purchase.

Out of Time

isaac e.j

Whispering, beckoning,
  "Out of sight, out of mind"
You are my saddest anecdote -
  An ending I cannot bear to write
The pause in a conversation
  The silence in the middle of the night

Listening, praying,
  "Absence makes the heart grow fonder"
But you are a stranger now and
I am a footnote in your Great American Novel

Shaky, shallow breaths and
Trying to conjure the colour of your eyes
Either left on read
Or granted two-word texts
Then your face appears
Smiling
On somebody else's timeline

A piece of me I left in the moving van
  A pain that patience could never dull

My Life With My Lover

Binod Dawadi

I used to love her so much,
I used to give her many gifts,
We used to travel far away,
As well as smile by looking at,
The faces of each other,
But one day she left me,
I become alone,
I wait for her for years,

But she never comes,
I don't forget that,
Happiest time my life,
Now also I want to be a child,
As well as do love with her,
My love is immortal and spiritual,
I am still waiting for her in my life,
As my precious time is already passed.

Phototrope

Janis Butler Holm

I remember the sun,
torrid and insistent,
how its ruthless radiance
dazzled the eyes.
Wave after wave,
the white, obliterating heat,
searing and bleaching,
dazing each thing
to staring incandescence.

Lying here, in the dark,
I know you're not the sun.
Above me, your skin
is dusky and cool.
Your eyes are shadowed
by something in the night.
So why am I thinking
of that brutish star?
Why am I burning, burning,
burning?

Preserves

Claire Thom

You keep a collection
of carefully arranged jars. One row

is bright red tomato sauce,
another sweet mandarin jam.

A small jar holds
spicy peppers, next to that

dried oregano. You tell me
your parents back in Italy

once spent an entire weekend washing,
peeling, slicing, boiling fresh

tomatoes from the market.
They filled twenty jars,

kept them in neat rows. Your father
died nine years ago,

your mother passed
last May.

I Want To Sleep In Your Pantry Just To Feel Something

Micah McCutchan

i unlock the door & somehow the smell of that
place frees you, it untangles you from all of those
tubes & pulls the needles from your hands. it
strips you of your hospital gown & like magic you
greet me in the doorway in your nightgown &
robe, smelling like hot coffee & insisting i come in,
so i do. your cheeks are no longer sallow, they are
round & pink & reassuring. your body holds mine
& i can't feel your bones anymore, all i feel is soft
warm flesh, familiar doughy arms wrapped
around me like a thick downy blanket. your eyes
sparkle again, like you have a secret to tell me,
something sweet to feed me, somewhere warm to
hold me. everything is how it should be.

i open my eyes & suddenly this apparition
vanishes & i am alone, so alone, standing in your
living room, just breathing in the settled dust of
your house. i run to the pantry & shut myself
inside, willing the smell of it to bring you back to
me, that version of you full of joy & life & free
from Is & rubber speckled socks & pain. maybe if i
stay in here the world outside will cease as i know
it, maybe if i stay in here i will magically become
seven again, eating goldfish crackers out of dixie
cups & watching cyberchase on the crispy carpet
with you. maybe if i sit on this holy ground & let
my tears drip on to the uneven floor it will be

enough for me to pull myself together & go visit
your emaciated body in that god forsaken hospital
bed again & hold it close to mine for as long as we
both have left

Memories Are Overrated

Jarvis Ottum

Some memories stick like spaghetti that someone
forgot to stir.
I can't tell where the noodles begin or end.

Other memories are like long-distance relatives.
It's hard to find them when you need them.
Easy to find them when it's too late.

Getting to some memories can be like going
through a challenging maze
with many dead ends and only one exit.
It may take multiple attempts to succeed for a
fuzzy prize.

The easiest memories to get to
are in a place called the Gap.
The Gap is like the ebbs and flows of the ocean.
The only problem with memories in the Gap
is that they're always changing.

Vestige

David Thomas

I remember happiness.
Running through my fingers
like the ripples of a dream upon waking
like the day before the rain.
I remember the face of a ghost pressed hard
against the window
the way that condensation ran from the blush of
her cheek.
The dour cries of mourning gulls
spilling down from the grey.
Still air and dragon breath cloaking us in the
diamond chill of the dead months.
I only ever wanted to be swallowed by the calm
absorbed by the perfection of a cold sunrise.
But dreams fade so quickly
racing back to the place where memories contort
into the crush of all that could have been.
A twisted orgy of hopes and despair
trying to fuck the balance back into place.

I remember summers that birthed fire in the
hissing grasses.
Pushing the current
waist deep against the flow.
Purity slowly evaporating from the glisten of our
skin as the zenith dropped its light
falling to earth in the cascading photon collective.
Too much wine
stars so bright they reflected in the glass waters

bats dipping wings in the mirror as we raised our
arms to the glorious night.
I remember the sine-wave frequencies of a
thousand spontaneous laughs
the crests that marked the the troughs.
The lasers
the volume
the immortality.
They were the smallest islands in the storm
keeping us safe from the uncertainty of evolution.
But we were never as safe as we thought.
I remember happiness
in the old friend that I never want to see again.
The blink of an eye
and everything dies.

I remember happiness.

I Am Memory

Jessica Wateski

You thought you lost or forgot me? How silly of
you. You know by now I show up randomly.
Sometimes I disguise myself. I come in waves of
happiness and sadness sometimes bringing
friends of anxiety, panic, hope, and love.

I never really go far and I like to pop in randomly
to ensure you don't forget me. I know there are
times you wish I wouldn't. I leave reminders
though, they come in pictures, smells, and sights.
Yeah, there are days you like me around because I
bring good feelings and vibes. And others you
wish you would be ridden with some mind
altering disease forgetting every part of what I
bring.

Hate me or love me. I am what makes you, you.
Without me, would you remember who you are or
were? You can't change me, I live in the past and
that cannot be undone, however, I can change you
because you learn from me.

A dangerous game we play over and over. So will
you let me stay? Or do I need to continue to
randomly pop in your mind and remind you of
who and what you are?

I'm not here to destroy you but make you
stronger. Some of me can stay in your past but I
won't ever truly leave. Use me. It's okay. You need

to learn. Enjoy my presence when I bring you good times. Continue to help me grow.

Tell others my stories because they're yours too!!

One day you might be looking for me, and you'll ask where did you go?

August's End

Giselle Linder

sometimes when the air is so quiet, I hear other
countries' thunder

the sounds of other lives won't stop seeping
through
slipping into the seams of dreams in restless sick
half-slumber

I stand in still air and listen for the sounds of
August's end
there are only church bells chiming and prayers
for something godsent

I know a little of how that feels
I was praying to be the godsend

the restaurant downstairs is closing up for the
summer
there was a woman there I worked up a sweat for
but I never worked up the courage to get her
number

oh well
there's always next year
so long as the business keeps itself from going
under

some are taking the high road
on their way out of town

I hung myself up high from one of two
skyscrapers
and said, if anyone is free and wants to hang out
I guess I'm still hanging around

with my feet dangling and my neck strangling
like a schoolgirl in love
I did try and scrape clean the sky
though my best efforts did nothing

perhaps even a vast blue can be afraid to hurt
and even more afraid to die

perhaps even a concept has cause to sigh

I don't know how I'm meant to make it to the end
of the month
when I'm not sure how to make it to the end of
today

I conceive of thoughts I can't share with anyone
and spill it all out in small talk just to find
something to say

I stand in the ghost town's lonesome street
and I give it all away

I give it all away

someone had better give me a penny for my
thoughts
if it's still tried and true that crime doesn't pay

and I'll try it and make sure it's true
if it just means I have something to do today

somewhere beyond conceivable distance lurks
August's end
further and further and further
down into the anaemic Thursday's journey we
descend

And I Think That Was Yesterday

adam Shove

And when I wake up,
Not always sure
If I remembered what happened,
If it were a dream
Or just a memory
That will take a moment to return to me.
A graphite pencil from the days
That I was able to draw,
Etched out what needed to be captured,
While latter day me
Was spanning the cosmos
For a reason why,
Not exactly an answer.
Do forgotten fragments of time
Span until infinity?
The backlight of time
And matter begins to take on the consistency
Of papier-mâché,
Then there were sirens and words
In the distance.
Now I'm too old to remember
If there's a level of relaxation
Between the first and last days of school,
I don't know if anything was all that,
Is something forgotten even all that?
I guess I'm looking for a word
That spanned from 85 'till.
A second hand rapture which was more
Than my bank balance could accept,
And the things that I can't ever remember

If they were said or not,
The shades of blue,
Flickered out into the ether,
The same as a flatline;
I guess I'm looking for a word
That spanned from 85 'till.

Change

L.M. Beatty

If you sit still as daylight wakes and pause,
expand your lungs with air sweet, full of peace—
moments, time stands still you almost forget
what it was to you, the meaning of life.
And yet in a breath suddenly it's clear:
a life lived well gives forth life abundant.
Such shame to waste a minute. Time's no thief.
The sun the moon the world spin ever on
but how we choose to spend defines true worth.
Life's value hung: measures of love and mirth.
To tip the scale, imagination joins
piled high with a generous heart. To give
of oneself is a precious gift received.
Quality shared, glimpse of magic revealed.
You are pure nature—Divinely-designed,
such beauty contained, bound for movement. Joy!
Such passion destined for sorrow and grief.
Creation created for creation.
Remember today your purpose, your role.
You're needed to nurture; help others grow.
It won't be easy, survival takes grit.
Only requirement: to try your best.
Empty your lungs release expectations
body at rest, soul on fire: you can't lose.

A Different Path

LaVern Spencer McCarthy

From youth, we walked together hand in hand,
our souls entwined, as roses are, in spring.
He took me to a far, enchanted land
sun-swept with joy that only love could bring.
We danced across the world without a care,
our happiness assured forever more,
for we had lives to live and dreams to share
until he found a road unseen before.
Why did I never hear the voice of fate?
I should have listened when the wind was high
above the distant mountain crest. Of late,
on dreary nights, I weep and wonder why

he lies asleep beneath a mossy stone
while I am left to find my way, alone.

How Can I?

Ndaba Sibanda

How can l draw upon the past events
and forget the naivety of our promises?

How can l eschew the music of grief,
the treasured voices still and smiles gone?

How can l draw upon the past events
and fail to frame my understanding

of the present? How can l fail to frame
my analysis of the behavior of people?

Remembering How You Forgot

Isabelle Palerma

When you forgot how to walk,
I found you a walker.
Nothing with the terrible tennis balls -
though that would let you slide into Paradise.
You thought them gaudy
and you were too much of a lady for something
like that.

I offered you my arm to lean on
and you smiled, saintly in your disease.
I smiled back, heartbroken in my malaise.
You told me I looked beautiful.
I guess the nursing home lighting hid
the tears, but nothing could disguise the dying.

Cruelty is the taste of ice cube knocking around
your mouth,
and finally sliding down
your throat
liquid melted from the hearth of your mouth.

You had forgotten how to chew, how to swallow
and we had seen the thin crepe paper
your sallow skin had become
and knew even if you'd forget,
we couldn't stand to remember all the saline IVs
hooked up to you.

Love was painting blue shadows on your eyelids
because

you told me you felt incomplete without it.

But then later, when cosmetics didn't matter,
love was our gentle coaxing,
"Inhale, exhale,"
because sometimes,
we couldn't stand to remember
that you had forgotten.

You had forgotten names
as you chased your finger
down old photographs.
Your hazel November eyes blurred.
(No one thought to remind you
to blink,
but she swore she saw you cry.)

You had forgotten how to breathe
and we watched as life withered out,
leaving behind a dry shell.

This is all out of order,
but what do timelines matter
(if all we do is forget)?

Eardrops

Swapna Sanchita

A pair of aubergine pearl eardrops sit
In a plastic box with a see-through lid.

The box lined with velvetesque red felt
And stowed away deep inside the locker
Of an old-fashioned rusty iron almirah
Whose paint is peeling off in scratches.

The preciousness of a pearl is in its colour
But these aren't gold, nor ivory white
Like the ones the fine ladies used to wear.
These are rarer, these deep purple pearls
That supposedly lie desolately forgotten
Secretly worn, dark nacreous keepsakes.

Let's Just Say

Kenneth Salzmann

Let's just say some memories
might hang in the air unnoticed
for a lifetime and then unexpectedly
come crashing down.
Let's just say you can find
yourself picking dream-shards
out of the carpet for years to come,
that uncertainty might be the only thing
a person ever can be sure of.
Let's just say she was the smartest girl
in school and I loved to hear her laugh.

Always

Peter Cashorali

Seeing Andy twelve years back
In the video Terrance made
I'd forgotten just how handsome
He'd been back then, or else not known,
So used to his unwasted face
That simply said here was Andy.
Reminded me of what I noticed
Back in high school when I read
Oscar Wilde's biography,
Saw how twelve or fourteen pages
In mid-book were all you needed
From his parents' wedding picture
To the photo of his tomb.
No surprise how brief it is,
Just the way we do things here.

What keeps coming from left field
Is the other side of things.
For example in my 20s
Briefly boyfriends, me and Andy,
Times we spent lasted forever
Which when things were good was great
But when not then not at all
So I sometimes walked on gold
And other times was chained in fire,
Heaven, hell, on daily basis
And not merely turns of speech.
Same thing when I first met Terrance,
There we were in paradise,
Lounging in eternity,

Which was great until it wasn't
And then suffering never stopped
So naturally we bailed on that,
Not again to see each other
Through all the ages of the world,
But met again and here we are
Till death, and then it's straight on through.
What's there for me to make of this?
That I'm fickle, have no time sense?
Think things last a billion years?
Or that here in human lifetimes
Is where everlasting lives,
Not unless or maybe later--
At home among the daily rounds,
Hardly noticed, no big deal,
Just the way we do things here.

Chain

Anita Howard

My mother wore her glasses
on a chain around her neck:
bifocals in smart rims
for any who might need
her scrutiny and sense of sharp proportion.

And I, with purple frames
on flimsy threads of beads,
now trail in those sure footsteps,
a blinking doppelgänger:
her contrary, tattered shadow.

Realm of Memories

Harjeet Khanna

In the realm of memories, whispers of the past,
Time's tender tapestry, woven to forever last.
Moments treasured, etched in heart's embrace,
A kaleidoscope of colours, a cherished mental
space.

Fleeting joys, like butterflies on the breeze,
Laughter and tears, woven amidst life's decrees.
Golden sunsets that kissed the horizon's glow,
And moonlit nights that cast a tranquil shadow.

Through seasons changing, memories remain,
A symphony of emotions, an everlasting refrain.
From innocence of youth to wisdom's grace,
Memories intertwine, a journey we embrace.

Each chapter penned in memory's sacred ink,
Love's sweet melodies, or hardships that make us
think.
Lessons learned, bridges burned, moments we've
sown,
The tapestry of memories, uniquely our own.

So raise a glass to moments cherished and true,
For memories are the threads that bind me to
you.
In the tapestry of life, they paint a vivid art,
A treasure trove of moments etched upon the
heart.

Ages

Henry Vinicio Valerio Madriz

Innocently step by step I timidly go.
From my loving mother's hands to
explore this world that is mine now.
Smiling at the odd winds that blow.

Playfully step by step I curiously go.
From my manly father's guidance to
interaction with the world amazed me.
Looking at an uncertain society's plea.

Challengingly step by step I sure go.
From my beloved family's roots to
conquer this world that shows creeds.
Showing off skills with human greed.

Solidly step by step I consciously go.
From my steady marriage's home to
study this world, with desire and pride.
Collecting memories and tears I cried.

Wisely step by step I peacefully go.
From my own living soul's voice to
fly away from dream to dream and so.
Resting my pace which became slow.

Joy, anger, love, and sorrow have paved the road.

When I Die

D.L. White

When I die, I want the wind to whisper goodbye in
your voice;
That tone like hot syrup dripping across freshly
woven silk,
Laced with roses and graceful virtue, tinted with
sinful milk.
I want your scent to echo in my final sips of
breath
As I inhale your lavender and golden odours one
last time,
The saccharine reek of your body spinning in my
mind.
I want storm clouds to release a furious chorus of
rain
Which pitters and patters the syllables of your
name,
Over treetops and rooftops, reverberating in the
lasts throbs of my eardrums.
I hope that the final touch on my skin is your soft
fingers
Tracing your adoration across my tired ageing
face.
I want the last sun rays to burn your image to my
retinas
So that my dying light is superimposed with your
majesty,
To then slowly fade to black with honorable
tragedy.
I wish that the last tear to fall on my face, traces
to my blue lips

And settles in my mouth, tasting of your sweet
caramel breath.
Oh, should my last heartbeat tick exactly as your
eyes guide,
Beckoning me softly to that final resting place in
the sky;
Me watching you watching me with angelic hues
drift away.
One ultimate time, I want your hands to clutch my
soul,
And your fingers to weave it around my dying
spine,
Creating a heavenly helix, rising up to my
cerebral cortex,
Where my spirit and psyche dance together,
defenceless
To the tune of your deliverance, bathed in your
brilliance,
Then dissipate away to the stars and heavens
above,
Tingling and thrumming with your perfect given
love.

This is my dedication to you, me and us; this will
be my dying wish.

I Remember

Ryan Kenny

I remember it just like it was yesterday,
I remember all the funny, important and
insightful things you'd say,
I remember the last conversation we had,
When I showed you my first car, and you asked
why I'd bought it for you, because you loved to
make me laugh,
I remember the way that sorrow flooded my
heart,
When I realised my life without you was about to
start,
I remember how much love was in the room when
your life came to it's end,
I still remember your smile, my hero, my
Grandad, my best friend,
But it pains me to know that things for you were
not the same,
It pains me to think you may not have been able
to remember my name,
It pains me to wonder if you're truly at peace now,
It pains me to think back to when I watched you
go,
It's so cruel, the torture you had to endure,
It's so cruel that you can teach me your lessons,
no more,
It's so cruel that you had that damned disease,
It's so cruel that the world must go on without
your improvised expertise,
Whether or not Alzheimer's did take your
memory,

It can never take away the childhood happiness
you gave to me,
It can never erase the times we spent together
making or mending things in your shed,
It can never erase the stories you'd make up
when you tucked me into bed,
It can never take away the joy we shared in so
many ways,
I'll remember that for the rest of my days.

Grief

Peter Cashorali

Let's take a moment and grieve for grief,
Because it doesn't last forever,
Grieve that the myrrh
Finally exhales the last of its perfume
And becomes harmless earth,
That the black cloth over the mirror
Is put away and light once more
Comes to drink, the judge takes off his robe
And retires from the bench.
The gravestone breaks,
The ground won't let go of the flower urn,
The vow dissolves once more into air and rejoins
the breeze.
Let's notice that the pyramids slowly turn to
vapor,
And the moon gains distance from the earth,
Will someday no longer eclipse the sun, and so
Observe the eclipse while we can,
Appreciate it if we can. Notice
How uncanny everything looks,
What light there is seeps in
From the horizon, so that farmlands
And highways and sky look like the underworld,
Where we wander or stand
And don't know what to do.
Like everything else loss
Doesn't last forever,
So treasure it while it's here.
We will mourn it when it's gone.

Hungry 2.0

D.L. White

I hunger,
for you
to still exist
from weeping lips
to fingertips.
As I breathe,
I dream your scent back
to my bloodstream.
For, I would want you
inside of me:
an extra organ;
a second heartbeat.

I could crave you, I suppose—
to the edge of eternity,
to the thinness of my sanity.
Wear you
like satin sheets,
weave each moment of loss
into muscle memory.
Hold your shape
as bitter-sweet tastes
behind my teeth.
My lips, unlicked,
muttering your absence
until my tongue tears to tatters
and I say your name
with blood in my mouth.

I could write of you,

the way Keats wrote of Brawne:
make you bloom
in poetry,
flush neon in prose,
and hope
my heart translates
to pen
in worthy ways.

I could
make atomic promises
and metabolic gestures,
swoon and fester
on this love
until... well, forever.

But you were no Romeo
and I am not Juliet.
We were not young lovers
destined to form
a death pact
to spite them all.

No.

We were longer-lovers
possessed by sands of time,
tangled up so tight
we forgot to stop
choking the life
from one another.

They say that love
is both the hunger
and the food:
if that is so,

I was famished
yet brim-filled by you.

my love
without a willing host
crumbles to starved dust—
In lieu of mortal flesh to touch
I'll settle
for your ghost.

Echoes

Zo Copeland

Surrounded by echoes
We are but ghosts in this life, too
Walking through walls of the past
Crossing boundaries lost to time
Our holographic forms
Following footsteps of old
Diverging into 'new' pathways
Of enemy descent
Leaning against lampposts
In the shadows
Of the workers that created them
Sitting on benches
On top of gravesites
On top of woodland
Mourning those we've lost
Yet still are here, hidden only by opacity
Fearing what we'll leave behind
Though we never really go
Walking down familiar streets
Right through the ghosts of loved ones
(same destination bound)
Surrounded by echoes
For our short time
As we fade into echoes ourselves

Have I been alive?

Norbert Góra

The future – uncertainty,
the obvious thing,
but oblivion of the present,
it is death in life.
You were
(or not)
here,
my own mind
is making fun of me.
It brings the images
in front of my eyes
and shoves them
deep in the head
(from the past?
I can't remember).
Step by step,
what am I going there for?
One thought persists,
have I been alive?

Gift in Secret

CLS Sandoval

Across from our sloped driveway
there was a dirt lot
just big enough to fit three or four cars
for those Mary Kay meetings
my mom held in our formal living room

Behind the dirt was a small pile of large rocks
which I would scale to go slightly up
to the cul-de-sac above

Going to the right
were the houses of the edge of Poway
leading toward Rancho Bernardo

On the left
was a huge sloping dirt driveway
blocked by a thin locked chain

I used to walk up that hill often

I could see the three dirt lots
that had been carved out
waiting for houses to be built on them

At the crest of the hill
was an even larger lot
with cans and bottles strewn about
sometimes the occasional empty pack of
cigarettes

My dad told me that people would camp up there
and I should be careful not to go up there alone
especially after dark

But on my 16th birthday
my first boyfriend took me there
we snuggled in a sleeping bag
fully clothed
just taking in the lights of the suburban town
below

He gave me a silver rope necklace that night
and my first memory of a boy giving me
something in secret

The street I once called home (Reprint)

K. D. Bowers

Many years ago,
I walked on this exact street as a child.
A place I called home;
I remember the joy, like looking at an old
photograph:
Sepia toned grins, roller-skates & soccer in the
road,
And the broken glass that made me the man I am
today.

Many years later,
The street that used to be filled
With children laughing and playing,
has moved on to some place new:
Office blocks, the country, buried beneath earth,
I don't know a single soul.
The street that I once called home
nothing but foreign to me.

We've Moved

Lawrence Miles

Do archaeologists hold requiems
for the sites they excavate?

As I sit in Tompkins Square
while a young man talks to himself on his cell
phone
I wonder if he has any idea
what Avenue A used to mean

Or are you supposed to let go of the past
as the breaths come deeper and harder

Old friends appear in the facades
of places active and dormant
I want to tell them how much they are missed
but I would only get silence in return

Watering holes now decayed Pandora's boxes
with the "We've Moved" sign torn in half

Paradise is now unlit and unmapped
appearing only through memory
as with the final moments of the pachyderm
before they lay down to sleep.

Nostalgic Adolescence

Vanessa Caraveo

Don't run so fast
But not so slowly either, so they don't reach you
You sing louder
But don't smile, you hurt your voice and your
throat
You look up
But don't forget look ahead

Your steps, my steps, are everything
Do not erase your tracks, because you will miss
them someday
Don't remove the marks from the door
Those brands that made mom and dad proud
Because you were taller, bigger, more grown
Because you were no longer a girl

I remember the stories, and keep those books
Enlarge your library if necessary, but not tires
Miracles and you will recognize them
They were part of your life, of the beginning,
Of the solidity that transformed you today into
what you are

Don't break your toys
They will make someone else happy
Polish your shoes
Those that no longer fit you, but made you walk
Iron your dresses
That today they do not enter a hand

You will find in all this more than objects that will
ever be from the past
You will find the stories that were not told out
loud
Photographs that were not captured on paper
The caresses that were not given with touch

Allow yourself to fall as many times as necessary
And always get up
Stronger
With more desire
And higher than yesterday

Wraiths

David Thomas

Was it ever anything more
than all those turbulent nights
being filled with the unattainable?
Introducing my frantic soul
to an out of body exposure
a plethora of agonies
as it thrashed against its chains.
We rode waves of sound
of light
of the breath that binds everything.
But somewhere in the pull of our burning gravity
the sky broke the land
and the sea devoured all that was left.
Here we smeared the stars
into streaks across the chalkboard sky
rendered fertile earth barren.
Such was our power.
Such was our destruction.
And we ran.
Ran with the ferals and the strays
seeking refuge
seeking peace
in doll's houses
in pillow forts.
Evading sleep without intention
as the storm surged in black and white.
We watched indigo relax into a still sunrise
through the cracks in our fingers
entranced in the devastation
that lay scattered through silent streets.

Each lonely home left standing
a monumental mockery
of everything we had desired.
A taunting metaphor of all our dreams.
And in the sanctity of our survival
we hung as wraiths in rags
touching cold skin
to the memory of our chaos.

Moments of Sand

Zo Copeland

Moments falling through space. Caught in the narrow neck between the chambers of the hourglass, held in the present just enough to freeze the frame. Memories bonding together in fluid motion to form a sea. So many wasted moments beneath the surface. A grain of sand here, a grain of sand there - seems inconsequential at the time. The more moments wasted, memories shrink to form a pond, deep but narrow. The more moments cherished, memories expand into endless horizons. Grain by grain, life passes, learning, in time, how to use it. Sands of possibility above weighing down into compacted shores below. Potential dispersed, moments spent. As my time runs out, my hourglass shatters; all that's left of me - a beach.

New York Next To Heaven

Giselle Linder

I was told to search for signs everywhere I went
But I see no angels

Rather, I see a mass of streets tangled together
like lovers and loose strings
And a temporary apartment in a temperate
Autumn

We shut our windows to the wind and wait to die
And make art and cups of tea to whittle away
the remainders of this grand life

October – I could kiss you

To the man who waits for me out in the world
I do and do not miss you

I do and do not wish myself upon you

No love letter serves as my lighthouse to bring me
home
Or lower me into the ground
Rather, I suspend myself like an acrobat
Threshold between two worlds
Counting the days until my next delayed train
arrives

I will weep over you as I watch the country pass
by
Boston-bound

Between now and then I press my gaze to the
sparkling harbour
Shaken by a train rattling over the tracks on its
last breath
Steady as a glass of cognac held in an anxious
hand
Loud as the last time we made love
When we both thought there was something left

In the bars I hand my wings into the coat check

I can't help but crave a desperate touch
I have spent October biting the hands of everyone
I have met

I stopped getting out of bed when I started feeling
that we were all waiting to die
And watching those molasses years trickling past
Bearing witness to our first murder of time

Yet here I am again, returning to some slim
excuse of a life

It's all been meaningless
Perhaps it was merely good fun

I keep threatening to walk out the door
But I was never good at having the final word
I never want this to be done

New York next to heaven

I catch the subway from Brooklyn to Manhattan
And walk the well-worn stones to the path of
Seventh

Soldier

Carella Keil

Originally published by Fragmented Voices 2023:
Inspire

i wonder: in that moment
did your life spin before your eyes
like a metal flower blooming outwards
each petal
shrapnel laced
jagged red diamonds exploding

did the red instant
remind you
the night you got high
babbled about losing your virginity
on a beach of vodka waves
the girl who
wrapped the ocean around you

cinnamon blossoms
    nailed into your skin
did you think of lag ba'omer
the bonfire you built
    hot as the horizon
your irises singed with smoke
how long did it take
to adjust to the dark

a third eye erupting
    scarlet
in the smooth white magnolia
of your forehead

did you remember
the way the wine gushed after the cork
toasting new years on a rooftop under the stars
you laughed as i
counted all the blackness in the sky

i wonder in that moment could you hear
the sizzle of shooting stars

RELEASED BY DARK THIRTY POETRY

ANTHOLOGY ONE
THIS ISN'T WHY WE'RE HERE
MORTAL BEINGS
POEMS THAT WERE WRITTEN ON TRAINS BUT
WEREN'T WRITTEN ABOUT TRAINS
CLOSING SHIFT DREAMS
DESIRE
ANIMATE
THESEUS AND I
I DON'T HAVE THE WORDS FOR THIS
CONVERSATIONS BETWEEN THE SUN AND THE
MOON
SLUT POP
JADED
I'VE BIRTHED AN IDEA OF YOU
BRUISES
CITY GOTHIC
LONG DIVISION
SAY HER NAME
LUMIN
VESTIGES
FALLING IN LOVE LOST
JUGGERNAUT
STIRRING TO LIFE
FORGOTTEN FRAGMENTS OF TIME

Leeds Library and Information Service
24 hour renewals
http://librarycatalogue.leedslearning.net
or phone 0845 1207271
Overdue charges may apply

Z E R O

Brian McCabe

Polygon

For George Lawson

First published in Great Britain in 2009 by
Polygon, an imprint of Birlinn Ltd
West Newington House
10 Newington Road
Edinburgh
EH9 1QS

www.birlinn.co.uk

ISBN 13: 978 1 84697 117 4

British Library Cataloguing-in-Publication Data
A catalogue record for this book is available on request
from the British Library.

Typeset in Great Britain by Antony Gray
Printed and bound by
Bell & Bain Ltd., Glasgow

Contents

COUNTERS

Counters	9
Throur	10
Seven	12
Nature Study	13
Minus Zero	15
Unprovable Theorems	17
Eleven	18
The Pronk	19
Facial Bones	20
The Fifth Season	21
The Seventh Sense	22
Triskaidekaphobia	23
Twin Primes	25
A Proof	26
The Undecidables	27
The Square Root of Minus Five	28
Chaos Theory	29
Two Quadrilaterals	31
1. *The Restless Square*	31
2. *The Unemployed Parallelogram*	32
Nine	33
Green Bottles	34
Mow	35

PERSPECTIVES

Chasqui	39
The Romans	41
Three Lives of Pythagoras	42
1. *A Free Slave*	42
2. *The Miracle of 63*	43
3. *The Future of Geometry*	45
Gematria	46
The Art of Remembering	47
Three Point One Four One . . .	49
Monsieur Probability	51
A Mere Girl	53
Two Infinities	54
1. *The Hypersphere*	54
2. *Infinity + 1*	55
Perspectives	56
Napier's Bones	58
The Professor and I	59
The Last Universalist	61
Enigma Variations	63
Blind Boy with Abacus	64
The Reckoning	65

ZERO

Zero	69
Notes	73
Sources and further reading	79
Acknowledgments	80

COUNTERS

Counters

Tiddlywinked into the inkwell,
– that thimble of pale enamel
like an egg's shell, nesting
in an ancient wooden eye –

they were the counters
and we counted them: 1,
2, 3 – but who was this
crosslegged abstraction – 4?

We added them into a column
which leaned towards infinity
before it spilled and scattered
its random pattern on the floor.

Soon they'd have us lined up
in columns: human logarithms
chanting an ugly prayer
to the god of multiplication.

The chaos we came from
would always be there –
whatever was done
with the counters.

Those bright buttons of colour
we placed on our tongues,
to taste the smoothness
the thinness of 1.

Throur

Today the government has announced
that a new number is to be introduced
into the existing number sequence
to help children to count beyond three.
The new number will come after three,
before four, and is to be called 'throur'.
Like other numbers, throur will appear
in sequence, notwithstanding magnitude.
So between thirteen and fourteen
there will be a new number throurteen.
Between twenty-three and twenty-four
there will be twenty-throur, and so on.
Strictly speaking this means that ten
or what we have called ten up till now
will become the eleventh number
or the number we call eleven.
The Minister for Arithmetic has said
that the ordinality of numbers
will remain unchanged. Cardinality,
however, may be affected adversely.
From now on the natural numbers,
the integers, the rational numbers
and the real numbers may not be
subsets of the complex numbers,
but separate objects isomorphic to
subsets of the complex numbers,
depending on how throur behaves.
There is to be a complete redesignation
of the times tables, the calendar, currency
– and everything else involving numbers.

The cost of the changes has been estimated
at throur-and-a-half throurillion pounds –
increasing the basic rate of taxation
to throurty-throur percent.

Seven

Never mind the planets the days of Creation
                              the ages of man
never mind the claptrap of the Apocalypse
the candlesticks the stars the trumpets
the spirits the horns the vials the plagues

Forget the deadly sins the kings of Rome
the heavens the wonders of the world
the last words of Christ on the cross
the son of the son and so on

My hooked finger beckons
and they all coming running
crying The magic number is about
to reveal its true mystery tell us tell us

And I do I say Go ahead
count the spots on the common ladybird
but they just don't get it they
just don't get it

Nature Study

Two by two we were lined up
like the animals for the Ark,
then hand in hand we walked
by the tall wall of the graveyard.

The teacher pointed out
the rogue egg in the nest
then told us to listen for
the first cuckoo of Spring.

In all our dog-eared jotters,
dressed in his speckled vest,
that fat, murderous imposter
would balloon his own name.

Our ladybirds' polka-dotted planets
would orbit the classroom, above
the perennial war between
deciduous and evergreen.

From the pond ripe with frogspawn
that reeked of an ancient birth
we gathered the curdled tapioca
and its slimed water in jars.

Those dots would hatch into commas
and grow legs to catapult them
over to the next page, vaulting
a leaning-tower of long-division,

the eruption of Pompeii,
the Wars of the Roses and
the heroic attempt at symmetry
of one dark, bivalve mollusc.

Minus Zero

Today we will be looking at:
the six-fold symmetry of snowflakes;
the spiralling motion of tornadoes;
the elliptical orbits of the planets.
We will also rediscover gravity,
Newton's laws of motion and – as we
do not appear to have one – reinvent
the computer from first principles
for number-crunching purposes
to extend the digits of *pi*.

Any questions?

Put away your calculators.
Take out your imaginations.
Now we'll tile a giant egg
using only two shapes of tile
and create a new classroom.
Your homework for tomorrow
is to find a formula for
the diminishing replication of fractals
with reference to the photocopy
of the map of Scotland I'll give out.

Any questions?

While you note that down
I'll come round and return
your colourful Möbius strips.
A neutral observer might think
I had forced you to demonstrate
new proofs from ancient theorems

or make lampshades out of flypapers.
Those with more than one side
have scored zero. Those which
don't join up: minus that.

Any questions?

Unprovable Theorems

His doomed eyes swam
in their fishtank lenses
like unprovable theorems
astonished to be trapped
in the ruthless medium of truth.

His cardigans could not contain
the stupendous parabola of his gut.
One button and – it followed –
one buttonhole had never met
in the random act of dressing.

How he wheezed and huffed
– as if some drastic mistake
had lodged inside his chest –
as he ridiculed our attempts
to classify the cubic curves.

How his cheek-tufts bristled
as he told us: 'Even Descartes
did better three centuries ago –
without the logarithmic tables
and without a slide-rule!'

When the dunderhead asked
'Sir, what are maths *for?*'
He pursed his lips, announced,
'Class, take ten squared lines:
mathematics is a *singular* subject.'

Eleven

*. . . has no connection with divine things, no ladder
reaching up to things above, nor any merit.*
                              – Petrus Bungus

The loneliest of long-legged bipeds,
he sulks mutely in his dim, narrow room.

Wishing to be ten again. Longing to be twelve.
Caught between two selves, a walking division.

He would make up a team with the others,
but he'd end up stuck between the posts.

He's grown out of his new long trousers;
his shirts are too tight around the armpits.

He compares his profiles in the mirror:
the one side is as boring as the other.

He knows he won't shine at anything;
he's been told he'll never reach the stars.

Eleven doesn't know who to turn to,
who to turn away from, who to love.

Something stutters in him to be born:
an ancient repetition, a second life.

The Pronk

Not the elegant diagonal symmetry of the Trot
and unlike the long, steady haul of the Pace
and hardly comparable to the Walk
and neither the skittishness of the Rotary Gallop
nor the quaint Transverse Gallop
and by no means the Canter
nor by any stretch of the imagination the Bound,
no, I know about them, I can do all of them.

The eighth quadrupedal gait is something else:
all four feet hit the ground
and leave the ground
together.

It has symmetry and beauty like the others,
but it is the most labour-intensive,
only to be used in emergencies
like a man firing a gun.

Like now. And now. And now.

Facial Bones

My facial skeleton has fourteen bones –
two sevens, a symmetry of mystery.

My maxima and mandible I need
to eat, drink, talk and kiss –
this last takes place after the others.
My orbits hold my eyes in place –
I am grateful to them for that.
Housed in the auditory bulba
are the bones of my inner ear –
who'd have thought I'd need
such an architecture to hear?
My nasal bones help me compete for smells –
there can be dignity in the ridiculous.
My formen magnum links brain with spine –
my mammal with my reptile.

It would all make perfect sense,
if not for my zygomatic bones:
all they do is curve and slant
from ancestral mirrors of water
and remind me of the mystery
my bones feel in their bones.

The Fifth Season

Everyone talks of the four
– none speak of the fifth.

Yet the fifth season stirs
its after-image in our memory
of a sun that glows dark
in a turbulent night sky.

It flits in and out of the year,
a mischievous impostor
mocking the snowdrops
with Spring snow of its own.

It makes the icicle burn us
like the tip of a lit cigarette. It brings us
the premonition of ice-floes
in the sun-blanched sand of the beach.

It persuades us of a summer in a summer
with mown grass and imminent rain,
an autumn leaking into a winter
with the dank undersides of bridges.

No one dares name the fifth
in case it might happen:
a dream put into words,
a notion made into dogma

and for fear its very name
might turn the world into
a rotten apple, to be tossed
back into the earth it came from.

The Seventh Sense

All talk of the sixth
or of the five
– none speak of the seventh.

The seventh sense can please itself
about what it apprehends:

the grey taste of a rainy day;
a premonition of an aroma;
what the caress once whispered
to a threadbare emotion.

The seventh sense can dress
in whatever it can dream.

But like the moth who dreamt
she was an emperor,
the seventh sense is never very sure
that it exists.

That's why it keeps reminding us
– with the kiss of a snowflake,
with the colour of a shout –
that we do.

Who knows –
even the diligent earth
might forget to go on turning
if not for the seventh sense.

Triskaidekaphobia

In order to help you overcome your fear
of what the Chinese call the Lord of Distress,
I suggest you try confrontation therapy.

So, on Black Friday, the day of Christ's death –
and yes, the thirteenth apostle betrayed him –
which also, as you've said, happens to be

you and your wife's thirteenth anniversary,
of which you live in so much dread,
we really have the ideal opportunity.

I want you to reserve a room in the Pyramid Hotel.
Unlike many, it has *the* floor – before you go in,
you must count them, from the ground –

and a room number 1313. On that date it is free
– I have checked – and you will find the rates
to be very reasonable indeed.

You must invite eleven guests – no more, no less.
The centrepiece at dinner should be a pineapple –
count the rows of scales sloping up to the right.

I want you to request that any flowers sent
have the requisite number of petals:
black-eyed Susans; corn marigolds; ragwort.

Read the Cabala to your guests – the section
about Paradise, the Heavenly Fountains,
the Gates of Mercy, the Rivers of Balsam.

This will be your phobia's last supper.
I'm afraid I can't – I'll be away.
Good luck and happy anniversary.

Twin Primes

They show up every so often,
these shivering refugees
sick with the infinite.

In their pockets they hide
stolen candles, calculators,
photocopies of each other.

After the search, we begin
the endless interrogation.
What are your names?

Where are you from?
Who do you represent?
What is your purpose here?

Words fail them: they can never
put a name to the catastrophe
they have left behind.

In isolation, they deny
all knowledge of their contact
and come out with the same alibi.

Only in the observation room
when they think they are alone
do they glance at each other

with something like pride.

A Proof

The data the computer was garnering:
thousands of pages of twin primes.
Sometimes we thought we had a pattern
somewhat like Riemann's, but not quite.
Then the next batch: it just didn't fit.
It was around that time that my wife left.
I felt numb to begin with, then number.
She told me she had other numbers
to deal with – and I knew that she did.
Then they stopped. As if the screen
had frozen, or the computer had crashed.
We made it print out its findings –
as if to verify them with our own eyes:
blank page after blank page.
I e-mailed my ex-wife, I asked her:
what could it possibly mean?
Did it mean the end of the twins?
She never e-mailed me back.
That was the question. It still is.
We have a research student check
that the screen is blank every day.
It always is, but we can't be sure,
and our funding is running out.
That's for sure: we can't be sure.

The Undecidables

We are not proven not proven we have never
been shown to be provable / non-provable
as the case may be we are not included
not included in such admirable certainties.
No we don't want to cause any trouble –
we're just bored theorems hanging about
on the streetcorner of current math thought.
Soon who knows something might happen
maybe one of our uncounted number
will be shown to be provable / non-provable
as the case may be. And he / she won't know
whether to feel proud or ashamed.
No doubt we'll congratulate him / her anyway
for being less undecidable than us.
In any case from then on he / she
will no longer belong no longer be one of us
if one can be said to be one of us – debatable.
We are not proven not proven we have never
been shown to be provable / non-provable
as the case may be we are not included
not included in such admirable certainties.
As we grow older our doubting faces
are stamped with the same question mark
but then we never die we never die

The Square Root of Minus Five

My grandfather – who smoked
himself to death in the fifties –
could count up to ten cigarettes.
Then he smoked them.

I can count up to five
but only in bananas.
I can add and take away
the bananas on the screen.

I know fractions:
my half-sister's second cousin
on her mother's side
always left half a banana.

In my dreams they multiply
on the branches as I swing
through the Fibonacci series.

If you ask me, the Golden Mean
owes a lot to the square root
of a bunch of minus five bananas.

Chaos Theory

A chaos lives in our house: she refuses to eat
when food is served; she eats when she's hungry,
or when she isn't, and eats what she likes.
To our relief and dismay
the doctor says she has a balanced diet,
the dentist that she has perfect teeth.

Her plans change from day to day.
When we ask her what they are
She's too busy doing nothing to say.
We don't know what to make of her
except that she's determined to be free.

For weeks she won't say a word, then
out it comes: a bloody, coloured eruption,
part confession part accusation all mixed up
in the incoherent logic of a tirade.

We daren't say a word. We know
the smallest thing can set her off:
one gentle word of well-meant advice
is taken as a closed fist, inside which
the butterfly's wings have been crushed.
That won't stop the tornado. Nothing will,
until it spirals into itself and is spent.
We'll pick over the catastrophe in its wake,
declare a state of emergency
and, with diminishing hope,
look for our survivors.

Still, when she smiles at us, she can
makes our fragile hearts falter.
Our theory is this: at some point
we will look into the eyes of chaos
and recognise the random pattern there
where flickers the order of the day.

Two Quadrilaterals

1. The Restless Square

There was a square who yearned
to become something else.

It stretched its legs to mimic
an elegant rectangle but
lost its balance, leaned over
in a perilous parallelogram.

It shrank to a rickety rhombus
before it sprang back into shape:
four equal sides and four
quite predictable right angles.

With a supreme effort then
it held its breath, drew in its corners,
swelled into a trembling circle,
stretched into an elegant ellipse

but the effort was so exhausting
that it fell asleep. When it awoke:
four equal sides and four
quite predictable right angles.

Then the square met another square
who was having a meeting for squares
all wishing to become something else
and together they found a way.

There was a cube who yearned
to become something else . . .

2. *The Unemployed Parallelogram*

When he leaned out of his window to observe
all the other four-sided hopefuls –
the rectangles the rhombuses the kites
the chevrons the butterflies the trapezoids

the squares of this world –
they called out to him 'Come and join us
we're forming a pattern with the triangles
and the hexagons might show up.'

He raised an acutely arched eyebrow
stretched his long legs scratched his angles
leaned on a sharp elbow and yawned.
He had another side to him.

He went to bed alone as usual
dreamt of concentric circles
of cubic curves of elegant ellipses
of shapes unbound by edges

of shapes that grew out of the plane
lay flat and flatter still until
he felt like a line a pure line
the line he had always been always would be
                                        it was endless

Nine

I was John Lennon's favourite number.
The number nine. Number nine. Nine.
I'm a stitch in time. A cat's lives.

I'm the heart of the helix – I whorl
from the rippling Sigma Codes
like a shell from its snail.

I with my spiralling eye
attract and distract predators:
mathematicians, with teeth.

Their arrows get lost in my target.
I hypnotise their wild formulae
into a dream of obedience.

In my shyness hides a mystery
you won't get from the primes,
the friendlies – or even the evens.

Children like me – they know
they can work out my times table
using only their ten fingers.

Green Bottles

I wanted the ten to stay ten.
I wanted the nine to stay nine.
I didn't want to think about
the wall with no green bottles.

Maybe I could make sure
that the bottle would not fall.
Maybe I could reason with
whoever knocked it from the wall.

Because it was very clear to me
that a bottle does not 'accidentally fall'
without the intervention of an arrow,
a stone, a stick or a ball.

But apparently this was not possible:
once that first green bottle had gone
the others had to follow, one by one,
until there were none.

So I counted them down
with the others, trying not to think
about a complete absence of bottles,
and a non-existent, stupid wall.

Mow

All those men who went to Mow,
went to mow a meadow –
were they mad?

Had nobody told them
that their job was pointless,
that the meadow was endless?

One thing is clear:
they did not go by choice.
They went because they were sent.

Maybe it is no co-incidence
that the place they mow in
is *called* Mow.

No doubt it was named after
its reputation: all that mowing
day and night, neverending.

The problem is the grass
keeps on growing and growing
and the owner despises daisies.

And so one man – deafened
by lawnmowers – shouts to his dog:
'I've had enough! Let's go!'

Then two men – the two
who followed him to Mow –
stop, wipe their brows and go.

Three men, four men, five men . . .
very soon there is an exodus
of men from the meadow.

Before leaving, the dog
cocks his leg at the infinite
and pisses a zero in the grass.

PERSPECTIVES

Chasqui

*ama suva, ama lulla, ama quella**

I am chosen by the Quipucamayoc the keeper
to be the runner from our village the last runner
to Cuzco itself where it is said dreams are lived
and the knots are stored like sacred treasure
it is undoubtedly an honour to be the last
along these long roads which have been laid
for this express purpose to direct me
through such vast lands strange and wild
with unnamed plants unnumbered beasts
towards order and the naming of all things
and more importantly the counting of them
perhaps at last even I will be named or counted
in any case I am chosen I have no choice

ama suva, ama lulla, ama quella

my father sacrificed a goat for me my mother
tied a necklace of tomatoes round my neck
a bladder of water on my back I will need them
the meat the fruit the water I am grateful for them
my duty to deliver the quipu may be rewarded
perhaps not in lima beans or maize but in coins
perhaps gold coins like the sun itself my father
has told me not to trade them for women
or boys but I may trade one for *chicha*

* Inca moral dictate: 'Don't steal, don't lie, don't be lazy.'

and drink to Pacha Mama Pacha Tata
Mother Earth Father Earth I am your servant
rewarded if not by the king then by the keeper
of the quipu or a servant of the keeper in any case

ama suva, ama lulla, ama quella

the green may be cattle the blue babies born
the yellow those tried or waiting to be tried
its threads those punished or pardoned
the orange those put to death I don't know
the white may be peace the red war
in any case it is not for me to understand
what each thread each knot represents
tens no doubt hundreds no doubt thousands
in the end all things must count and be counted
I was chosen because I am a good runner
I have faith I will be rewarded if not in coins
I will be sacrificed and my death recorded
in any case it won't have been for nothing

ama suva, ama lulla, ama quella

The Romans

Listen up. This is how
We're about to count from now on.

We got a one: I. We got a five: V.
We got a ten: X. We got a fifty: L.
We got a hundred: C. We got a five hundred: D.
Also plus we got a thousand: M.

That's it. That's all we need.
The fuck with dealing out letters
to two three four six seven eight nine,
eleven twelve thirteen etcetera.

Those motherfuckers can go eat shit.
The rule is: you add the little fish
if it comes after the big fish
because the big fish eats it, right?

When the little fish comes before
the big fish, you take it away –
on account of the big fish ain't
ate it yet, okay? Any questions?

Whaddya mean howdya write
one hundred and sixty-four?
Am I talking to myself here?
CLXIV. Dumbfuck.

This means Tony the Scribe
only needs to know seven letters
to run any number we tell him.
Okay, let's go eat Chinese.

Three Lives of Pythagoras

1. A Free Slave

Understand this, Zalmoxis,
I bought you in order to free you.
Let me show you the hieroglyph
which explains the flow of rivers.

You must join my semi-circle.
The apprenticeship is five years
of silence, worshipping Apollo
and eight hours Geometry a day.

Here is what you do: go to Thrace.
Hide in an underground chamber.
I will follow you. You will hear me
singing the music of the spheres.

That's your cue: rise from the dead.
Don't worry about the town elders –
they will express surprise and wonder.
Then I will begin my discourse:

This is my sacred discourse.
Everything is part of one soul.
The gods are stars and numbers.
We should not eat animals, or beans . . .

2. The Miracle of 6³

We were hauling in the catch
when he appeared on the shore.
He was something else to look at:
the trousers, the long hair, the turban.
He didn't look like a Greek to me.
More like an Egyptian or a Persian.

When he showed us his golden thigh
and said he was the son of Apollo
I thought I should pay attention.
I listened to what he had to say –
this prophet of earthquakes,
this charmer of triangles.
He told us we should sacrifice
to Aphrodite on the *sixth* day.
Six was perfect, he said – the child
of its divisors: one, two and three.
Moreover it was circular, since
all its marriages ended in six.

It didn't make any sense to me.
There were only five of us there –
unless you counted Pythagoras.
To give him his due he predicted
the size of our catch. Mind you,
he did supervise the count.

When he bade us set the fish free,
we did. This shaman from Samos,
this cave-dweller who heard
the pure music of the spheres –
his fame has come before him –
who knows what powers he has?

When he paid us for the catch
we'd squandered, he said,
'Two hundred and sixteen.
Six *cubed*, six to the *third* power –
or the number of years between
your death and your rebirth.'

We nodded and we applauded.
He was a very good speaker.
I mean – he knew when to stop.
I was coming to the miracle.
The miracle was the fish:
during the count, none died.

Is this all the bread there is?
Let me share it out equally.

3. *The Future of Geometry*

Out on the boat with the brotherhood
he had his right-angled triangle
and his table of opposites with him.
And his kithara. He'd demonstrated

that when you stretch the strings
in a simple ratio 2:1, 3:2 or 4:1
they'd make consonant notes
when they were plucked.

He was also going to show them
what he'd found out in Babylonia –
when the flood waters had receded,
the demarcation of the fields:

that in a right-angled triangle
the square of the hypotenuse
is equal to the sum of the squares
on the other two sides. Always.

Trust that loudmouth Hippasus
to bring up the square root of two.
Him and his 'irrational' numbers.
They're *expressible,* he'd said.

So be it: the boat would return
to the shore with one student less.
(Some sacrifices were necessary
for the future of Geometry.)

Gematria

Pope Innocent IV
signed the papal bull
authorising the use of torture
in the Spanish Inquisition
and finished his breakfast.

The sun came up as usual
according to certain laws
– religious or mathematical,
did it really matter which?
In any case it had no choice.

Even if what they were saying
was true: so his cryptograph
was the number of the beast
in Revelations 13:18 – the case
against him was absurd.

An agitated cardinal entered
bearing a message from Batu
– that grandson of Genghis Khan –
declaring war and telling him
that his heart would roast in hell.

Tell him he can kiss my ring.
There was nothing like a war
to spread the word of God.
Today's sermon would be:
Prester John destroying Islam.

The Art of Remembering

Giordano Bruno 1548–1600

Gentlemen of Rome, with respect, for many years
while in Paris, I taught the Art of Remembering.
And as I quite clearly remember saying
to your honourable colleagues in Venice:
retract what?
          If this inquisition would inform me
what it is you would like me to retract
I will gladly do so, though you must agree
that the truth is not the truth because
the majority believes it, and must be
for any honest man,
                    unretractable.
You have your methods of enquiry
and I have mine.
          A moving Earth
does not contradict our Christian beliefs.
True, the Catholic, the Calvinist, the Lutheran
– I believe they must learn to co-exist –
all have banished me.
          I am not in this business
of separating faith from knowledge, belief from truth
to make friends, or to gain a chair at Padua –
I have no envy of Galileo the Copernican;
I am sure he deserved it more than I –
and yes, I did flee Naples, Rome, Geneva,
Oxford, London, Paris.
          But gentlemen, may I
remind you: I was invited to return to Italy

47

as the guest of the esteemed Moncenigo,
who then furnished you with these accusations.
(The Earth does indeed seem to stand still
and the sun to revolve around it; even these
cosmic appearances can deceive us.)
I understand.
                    You must heed Pope Clement's demand.
Perhaps your fear on passing judgement on me
is greater than mine in receiving it.
                                    So be it.
In any case you will remember this:
just as this entire earth, this rolling star
renews itself, transforming all its parts,
I am ready to become my altered state.

The spectators will come to observe me
but I too will observe them, for
this universe is infinite, in flux,
and the observer is always the centre.

You may gag me now. Take me to the stake.

Three Point One Four One Five Nine Two Six Five Three Five Eight Nine Seven Nine Three Two Three Eight Four Six Two Six Four Three Three Eight Three Two Seven Nine Five Zero Two Eight

Ludolf van Ceulen 1540–1610

The final item is the gravestone
of Ludolf van Ceulen of Leyden,
seventeenth-century mathematician.
He spent most of his life
calculating the value of *pi*
by the Archimedes method
to the first . . . ah, thirty-five digits.
They are engraved on the stone
beside the date of his death: 1610.

A decade later his painstaking work
was obsolete. This is his stone.

May we start the bidding at three?
We have it from the gentleman
in the hat from the University of Texas.
Three thousand one hundred dollars
from the bidder on line from Leyden.
From the man in the hat from Texas
we have three thousand one hundred
and forty dollars. From Leyden
we have one hundred and forty-one.
Three thousand one hundred and
forty-one dollars and *fifty* cents
from the man in the hat from Texas.

From Leyden we have fifty-*nine* cents.
Any more bids? Sold to the bidder
who is on line from Leyden! So:
the tombstone of Ludolf van Ceulen
is returned to the place of his death
for three thousand one hundred and
forty-one dollars and fifty-nine cents.
Or the value of *pi* to the sixth digit.
Cheap at the price, considering.

Monsieur Probability

Abraham de Moivre 1667–1754

You must remember old Abe de Moivre.
Handsome Frenchman. The nose not quite aquiline
but a nose of note nonetheless. The lip curled.
in the manner of the French, as if prepared
to dismiss any poorly expressed idea.
The facial bones gaunt, but refined.
Always in Slaughter's. He used to slaughter me
at chess – for a groat, or a cup of coffee.
I didn't grudge him it. He'd fallen on hard times.
Had to teach the brats of the nobility.
Always carried a few pages he'd cut
from the *Principia* wherever he went.
If you needed to know the odds on anything,
de Moivre was your man. Monsieur Probability
we called him. His *Doctrine of Chances*
became known as the Gambler's Bible,
though he didn't like to hear it called that,
him being a devoted Protestant.
Not that he'd had much luck:
thrown in jail by Louis the Fourteenth
when they scrapped the edict of Nantes.
After that he came to St Martin's Lane.
Newton himself would consult him,
take him home for a bit of discourse.
It was him got de Moivre that commission
to decide who came up with the Calculus –
Leibniz or Newton, that great debate.
The Society was taking no chances.

That was the last he saw of Lady Luck.
Reduced to advising the likes of me
on my chances of winning a wager.
Always poring over his figures he was,
almost went blind towards the end.
Used to sleep over twenty hours a day.
They say it was the somnolence killed him.
He could always tell the outcome of anything,
even foretold the day of his own death:
said he slept a quarter hour more every day
so he worked out that when he slept for twenty-four
that would be the day – and he was right.
And what, sir, are the chances of that?

A Mere Girl

Sophie Germain, 1776–1831

You were a child of the revolution
and a revolution yourself: your passion
sealed in your father's library. Archimedes,
too intent on reading a figure in the sand
to heed the question of a soldier, was speared
– at a slightly acute angle – through the heart.
Even your parents could not deter you
by confiscating light, heat and clothes:
with smuggled candles, wrapped in blankets
you warmed your mind with calculus,
cut your hair and dressed as a man,
replaced a drop-out from the Academy.
'The heretofore indifferent work of M. LeBlanc,'
the professor wrote, 'has undergone a transformation.'
Your talent was too conspicuous. The game was up:
you were unmasked as a mere girl.

The pitch for your biopic came back
from the producer: 'no love-interest'.
There was just the dismissive Monsieur Poisson,
– your rival in the field of *Elastic Plates* –
who stretched and distorted your truths
till they snapped – yet the trembling curves
of the Eiffel Tower held fast. On one of them,
where your name should be, is *Poisson.*
You are a street in the 14th *arrondissement*,
a crater on Venus, and a mind that is still
gently quivering through the twin primes.

Two Infinities

1. *The Hypersphere*

Georg Friedrich Bernhard Riemann 1826–1886

The year is 1854. In his study
– cluttered or uncluttered, depending
on the *mathematical* meaning of 'clutter' –
Georg Friedrich Bernhard Riemann
reviews the concept
of the hypersphere.

He sees no reason why
there shouldn't be a duoverse,
a triverse, a quadiverse, a cinqueverse . . .
No reason why time should not loop
and join up in eternal recurrence.

His wife enters, bringing him tea.

He watches her walking from the door
to the table. Will she ever get there?
But she always does, puts down
the tray, and asks him if he is well.

He nods to her. There is eye-contact.
They have a brief conversation.
All this has taken place before.

When she leaves, she closes
the door. And he thinks of Zeno
trapped in that room of his,
that room he could never leave.

2. Infinity + 1

August Ferdinand Möbius 1790–1880

In 1858, in Paris,
August Ferdinand Möbius
paces the floor, trying to think
of a topic for the competition.

Perhaps he could discover
a pattern to the twinned primes?
No: it must have been done.
He needs something better.

August Ferdinand Möbius
runs his five elegant fingers
through the complex formulae
of his luxurious brown hair.

He needs to smoke a pipe
but he has run out of tapers.
He tears a strip of his paper
to take a light from the fire.

Instead he twists it, joins it.
It has one side and one edge
and appears to be neverending.
The implications are endless. ·

If only the closing date wasn't
the day after the day before
tomorrow.

Perspectives

Mary Somerville 1780–1872

The strain of abstract thought, her father feared,
might injure her tender female frame. It did not.
It was more the needlework, the pianoforte
at Miss Primrose's Boarding School for Girls
in dreary Musselburgh which fettered her spirit.
When she left, she said she felt like
a wild animal escaped out of a cage.
Then there were the endless parties
and balls and concerts and visits – all
those 'harmless flirtations' bored her stiff.
The private painting lessons at least
dealt in perspective, the *Elements* of Euclid,
and Nasmyth, with his painter's eye, saw
that her talent was less for landscape
than plotting how the vanishing point
might move with the picture's spectator.
He referred her to Leonardo, Brunelleschi.
Meanwhile she did her brother's algebra
by the light of a hidden candle in her room.
When it had sputtered and gone out,
she worked by the light of the moon.
Out there, the night sky seethed with riddles
and she ached to explore its perspectives,
its vanishing points, its spectator.
What she couldn't work out today
she would understand in the morrow.
Soon something had to be done
to bring about the rights of women

to study the mechanism of the heavens,
for example the orbit of Uranus.
What if its perturbation were caused
by a hypothetical planet? What then?
How difficult it was to be a young lady
and midwife to the birth of Neptune.

Napier's Bones

John Napier 1550–1617

It was no wonder that the servants at Gartness
were loath to speak their master's name; it was itself
a rum conundrum: Napeir, Nepair, Neper
Napare, Naper, Naipper. Lord Merchiston it was.
They had seen the castle fields fertilised
with common salts for the manure
sprout corn and crops of all sorts. More than once
at his bidding they had shut down the mill
to silence not the cascade – which, he said,
soothed his thought – but the clack of the wheel
which interrupted the flow of his calculations.
They had heard him speak with Auld Nick
of spherical triangles, of tables made from numbers.
One reported that he could make a thing occur
by predicting it would not. She heard him say:
'Mr Briggs will never come now' whereupon,
in a coach and horses all the way from London,
who do you think should draw up at the gate?
Some even swore he could make numbers
multiply themselves; those who'd seen his 'bones'
cut from ivory and marked with numbers
like the keys of some satanic piano
dared not doubt that fearful fact,
for at full moon they had often watched
their lord go abroad into the night
wearing but his nightgown and his cap
and under his arm – for they knew not what
dark necromantic act: a cockerel, black.

The Professor and I

A professor at the Sorbonne, no less,
and a member of the Académie des Sciences!
But he fell for it every time – he *wanted* to believe
that Pascal wrote to Newton, claiming the theory
of universal gravity. If he'd checked the date
he'd have known that Newton was ten,
but you see, it made the discovery *French*.
Of course I threw in others to beguile him
from Leibniz to Descartes and Louis XIV.
Cleopatra, Julius Caesar, Alexander the Great
– even those three wrote in perfect French!
Galileo caused me a problem, because
he pointed out that he'd gone blind.
I had to write another, hinting that he was
pretending, to outwit the Inquisition.
There was no end to my invention, and no end
to his hunger for the stuff. He would tell me
what most interested him, ask if I knew of any
letters by Plato to Aristotle. I doubt it, I'd say,
then go away and write the things to order.
I was drawing on the extensive collection,
of course, of a great and illustrious person
who did not wish to make himself known.
The oldest trick in the forger's ancient book.
Mind you, I did my homework: every day
after lunch – at the Café Riche when I had money –
I'd sit in the Imperial Library reading the history,

then I'd pen the letter, using inks unique to me
and old parchment aged with fire and tea.

As I told the court – the patriotic old fool
took 'Pascal' to the Académie! – it wasn't easy money.

The Last Universalist

Jules Henri Poincaré 1854–1912

Poincaré. The name was enough
to take me back to Magny.
I thought it must be a namesake.
I had no idea he was a man of the mind.
The obituary called him
'the last universalist'.
Then I read 'Inspector of Mines' . . .

I was off-duty, asleep in my bed
when the roar of it woke me:
like thunder underground.
There was no choice but to go.

The first body I found:
burned black and still aflame.
Beside him, his lamp.
I took the jacket off my back
and put the fire out.
Then Poincaré was there.
Strange to see a smart young man
wearing suit and tie, pince-nez,
in the midst of catastrophe,
taking measurements, testing
for firedamp. I gave him the lamp.
Afterwards, I read his report:
'Lamp 476 had been damaged by a pick' –
my friend Baudoit.
I had issued that lamp to him.

Poincaré recommended my reward.
He said if I hadn't doused those flames
there would have been another inferno.
I gave it to the widows, to the orphans.

Only this year, Poincaré said
a spark had been enough
to ignite the mix of gas and air,
and refused to describe the horror.

Enigma Variations

Alan Turing 1912–1954

It is for those who see an unbridgeable gap
to say just where the difference lies.

As a boy scrambling in the heather
he heard wild bees buzz past,
studied their flight-paths,
plotted the intersection,
and found the nest.
His contribution to the picnic
was more the appliance of science
and his parents' astonishment
than the honey he brought back.

At school, in *Natural Wonders*
Every Child Should Know, he read:
'For, of course, the body is a machine.'
Something clicked into place
and went on clicking until
his brain became its own machine,
and the machine began to think
of another machine which could think,
make decisions, change its function
a machine which would be able to do
the work of any other machine
and above all, it would be jolly well able
to slaughter all his housemates at chess.

And then there was the other
unsolvable problem of sex.

Blind Boy with Abacus

Between his spidering fingers
each stone is a cool calculus.
In the brouhaha of the market
where they sell cheap calculators
his blindness is the blessing:
he is left alone with his stones.
Occasionally the stall owner
asks him to make an addition.
He does it without hesitation
in his head – the abacus being
fully occupied in working out
how Riemann's incorrect statement
of Drichlet's principle, corrected,
leads to the calculus of variations –
and calls out: 'Twenty-nine rupee!'

The Reckoning

This is what you have to do:
write their numbers in this book.

The taking away of the living,
the adding up of the dead –

a strange arithmetic isn't it?
They were numbers in life too.

Something I've noticed: orifices.
All men have eleven.

Twelve, if you count the navel.
Women have thirteen – unlucky.

This one is nine-nine-seven.
Her only significance now

is her number: the last prime
before a thousand.

I don't suppose it matters to her
that she has that distinction.

You'll get used to it. I did.
Go on from where I left off.

After the next two, of course,
you'll need another column.

Now I have to go over there
to count the living.

ZERO

Zero

it was already there
turning in the ancient dark

o

umbret et encombre
nameless in its nothingness

o

when the earth was without form and void
and darkness was upon the face of the deep

o

the primal womb of all things
before light before life before number

o

sufficient unto itself
its halo the crown of that chaos

o

the unrecognisable
the unnumber

o

Long after men had learnt
to count on our fingers and toes
or with pebbles and shells and beads
it remained unseeable, uncountable, unacceptable.
Even when its shape – the depression left in the sand
when a counter is removed – became etched on the eye
and it was given its names:

      shunga
      xok
      ouden
      null
      nil
      galgal
      sifr
      zero

      0

And even when we found that this cipher had its uses
– 108 cows meant something different from 18 cows –
then found ways to write it – an empty oyster shell,
the space between notches in clay, the double-notch,
the unknotted string of the *quipu*,
the circles carved on a tablet of stone
to calculate the size of the garden
to grow garlands for the temple at Gwalior –
still its nature remained elusive,
a ripple appearing then disappearing.
Even when it came into its own
in *The Opening of the Universe*
and Brahmagupta wrote
a debt minus zero is a debt,

a fortune minus zero is a fortune
it confounded him still:
zero divided by zero is zero.
Perhaps it will outlive us at last:
implacable, inscrutable to the end.

o

when darkness will again be upon the face of the deep
and the earth will be once more without form and void

o

umbret et encombre
nameless in its nothingness

o

turning in the ancient dark
it is already there

Notes

Twin Primes

Twin primes are pairs of prime numbers (numbers which are only divisible by themselves and 1) separated by only one other number, for example 17 and 19. The question of whether there exists an infinite number of twin primes has been one of the great open questions in number theory for many years.

Chasqui

The Incas developed a method of recording numerical information which did not require writing. It involved coloured strings called *quipu*, knotted to represent numbers. Each colour had several meanings, including abstract concepts, such as peace or war, and concrete things, such as livestock or people. In addition to colour-coding, another way of distinguishing the strings was to make some strings subsidiary, tied to the middle of a main string rather than being tied to the main horizontal cord.

The Incas had no written records and so the *quipu* played a major role in the administration of the Inca empire. The Inca king appointed *quipucamayocs*, or keepers of the knots, to each town. Larger towns might have had up to thirty *quipucamayocs* who were essentially government statisticians, keeping official census records of the population, the produce of the town, and its animals and weapons. This and other information was sent annually to the capital Cuzco via an official delivery service consisting of relay runners, or *chasqui*, who passed the *quipu* on to the next runner at specially constructed staging posts.

Three Lives of Pythagoras

We should not eat animals, or beans . . .
Pythagoras and his followers were vegetarian, and did not
eat beans because of the bean's resemblance to a human
foetus.

Six was perfect, he said . . .
6 was considered a 'perfect' number by Pythagoras because
its divisors, 1, 2 and 3, add up to 6. It is also 'circular' in the
sense that all its powers end in 6 (6 x 6 = 36; 6 x 6 x 6 = 216;
6 x 6 x 6 x 6 = 1296 etc.)

what he'd found out in Babylonia . . .
Pythagoras travelled to Babylonia, where people for
centuries had used the 3–4–5 triangle to demarcate fields
with right angles after the floodwater of the Nile had
receded. In that sense Pythagoras did not discover it, but
realised its importance.

An irrational number is one which cannot be represented
as a fraction or as a finite, non-repeating decimal. For
example, *pi* is an irrational number, as is the square root of
2. Hippasus, one of Pythagoras' students, is said to have
first discovered irrational numbers. It is also said that he
made this discovery while out at sea and was subsequently
thrown overboard by his fellow Pythagoreans. Hippasus's
discovery posed a very serious problem to Pythagorean
mathematics because it shattered the assumption that
number and geometry were inseparable, a foundation of
their theory.

Gematria

Gematria is a type of number mysticism which associates numbers with a word by adding up numbers attributed to its letters. The name 'Innocentius Papa' (Pope Innocent IV) has the number 666 – the number of the Beast in Revelations 13:18.

The Art of Remembering

Giordano Bruno not only argued for a moving Earth, but also that the universe was infinite and contained other stars like the sun and other planets like Earth. He knew that this contradicted the Biblical version of the universe, but he put forward the same argument as Galileo would some years later, namely that the Bible should be seen as providing moral teaching, not the teaching of physics. He was sentenced to death by the Roman Inquisition for his beliefs and was burned alive at the Campo de' Fiori on 17 February 1600.

Two Infinities

A hypersphere is a sphere having more than three dimensions. Since the early twentieth century, mathematicians have used this idea of a higher-dimensional sphere to describe a universe in which time is the fourth dimension.

Zeno / trapped in that room of his . . .
One of the many paradoxes that Zeno put forward was that of a man wishing to travel from A to B. Before he can get to B, he must travel halfway there. Before he can get halfway there, he must travel a quarter of the way there. Before getting a quarter of the way, he must travel an eighth; before an eighth, a sixteenth; and so on. This description requires the man to complete an infinite number of tasks, which Zeno maintained is an impossibility.

Perspectives

In *The Connection of the Physical Sciences*, which was published in 1834, Mary Somerville discussed a hypothetical planet perturbing the orbit of Uranus, which may have prompted John Couch Adams to investigate and subsequently discover the planet Neptune.

Napier's Bones

John Napier's practices often appeared strange to his contemporaries and, given the superstitious age in which he lived, rumours circulated that he was in league with the powers of darkness. According to Mark Napier, one of John Napier's descendants, he deliberately played upon the primitive beliefs of his servants by walking out at night wearing his nightgown and cap and carrying a cock which he had covered in soot.

The Professor and I

Michel Chasles was a professor at the Sorbonne and a member of the Académie des Sciences. The forger who speaks in the poem is Denis Vrain-Lucas. Using old paper stolen from libraries and special, handmade inks, Lucas forged letters by Pascal, Galileo, Descartes, Newton, Louis XIV and many others. Chasles bought thousands of manuscripts from Lucas between 1861 and 1869, some of which purported to be part of a correspondence between Newton, Pascal and Boyle. Chasles presented the letters to the Académie des Sciences in 1867 maintaining that they proved that Pascal was the first to propose the universal law of gravitation, and not Newton. Chasles argued strongly that the letters were genuine. However Vrain-Lucas was tried in 1869–70 and found guilty of forging the documents; and Chasles had to appear at the trial.

Zero

the temple at Gwalior:
The first (dated and agreed by all to be genuine) record of the Indian use of zero was found on an inscription on a stone tablet, dated 876. The inscription concerns the town of Gwalior, 400 kilometres south of Delhi, where a garden was planted. It measured 187 by 270 hastas and was designed to produce enough flowers to allow 50 garlands per day to be given to the local temple. Both the numbers 270 and 50 inscribed on the tablet are denoted almost as they appear today, although the 0 is smaller and slightly raised.

Brahmagupta wrote:
The Indian mathematician and astronomer Brahmagupta (598–668) attempted to give the rules for arithmetic involving zero and negative numbers. He gave the following rules for addition which involve zero:

> The sum of zero and a negative number is negative, the sum of a positive number and zero is positive, the sum of zero and zero is zero.

Subtraction was a little harder:

> A negative number subtracted from zero is positive, a positive number subtracted from zero is negative, zero subtracted from a negative number is negative, zero subtracted from a positive number is positive, zero subtracted from zero is zero.

He then said that any number when multiplied by zero is zero, but struggled when it comes to division:

> A positive or negative number when divided by zero is a fraction with the zero as denominator. Zero divided by a

negative or positive number is either zero or is expressed as a fraction with zero as numerator and the finite quantity as denominator. Zero divided by zero is zero.

Brahmagupta was certainly wrong in claiming that zero divided by zero is zero. However it was a brilliant attempt from the first known person to attempt to extend arithmetic to negative numbers and zero.

Sources and further reading

The MacTutor History of Mathematics Archive, St. Andrews University

http://www-groups.dcs.st-andrews.ac.uk/~history/

Cecil Balmond, *Number 9: the search for the Sigma Codes* (Prestel, 1998)

David Blatner, *The Joy of Pi* (Penguin, 1997)

Peter Gorman, *Pythagoras, A Life* (Routledge & Kegan Paul, 1979)

Denis Guedj, *Numbers: the universal language* (Thames & Hudson, 1998)

Reuben Hersh, *What is Mathematics, Really?* (Jonathan Cape, 1997)

Robert Kaplan, *The Nothing That Is: A natural history of zero* (Oxford University Press, 1999)

Mario Livio, *The Golden Ratio* (Review, 2008)

Simon Singh, *Fermat's Last Theorem* (Fourth Estate, 1997)

Ian Stewart, *Does God Play Dice?* (Penguin, 1990)

Ian Stewart, *Nature's Numbers* (Weidenfeld & Nicolson, 1995)

Acknowledgments

Acknowledgments and thanks are due to the editors of the following publications: *Chapman*; *The Scottish Book Collector*; *The Scottish Review of Books*. The author would also like to thank the the Fondation Chevillon for a Robert Louis Stevenson Fellowship in 2007 and the Scottish Arts Council for a Writer's Bursary in 2008, both of which helped him to complete this collection.